Understanding the Dreams You Dream

Biblical Keys for Hearing
God's Voice in the Night

Ira L. Milligan

Treasure House

An Imprint of
Destiny Image® Publishers, Inc.
P.O. Box 310
Shippensburg, PA 17257-0310

"For where your treasure is,
there will your heart be also." Matthew 6:21

ISBN 1-56043-284-5
(Previously ISBN 1-56043-761-8)

31 32 33 / 12 11 10

For Worldwide Distribution
Printed in the U.S.A.

This book and all other Destiny Image,
Revival Press, MercyPlace, Fresh Bread,
Destiny Image Fiction, and Treasure House books
are available at Christian bookstores
and distributors worldwide.

For a U.S. bookstore nearest you,
call **1-800-722-6774**.
For more information on foreign distributors,
call **717-532-3040**.
Or reach us on the Internet: **www.destinyimage.com**

For information concerning having a seminar
conducted in your church, contact Ira at:

**Servant Ministries
P.O. Box 1120,
Tioga, LA 71477**

Dedication

This book is dedicated to my patient and loving wife, Judy.

Appreciation

I wish to express my heartfelt thanks to those precious saints of God who have supported us with their prayers and substance to allow us to give ourselves wholly to prayer and to the ministry of the Word.

All references to Greek or Hebrew word definitions, with the exception of proper names, are from *Strong's Exhaustive Concordance* (James Strong, LL.D S.T.D., Thomas Nelson Publishers, 1990). The meanings of biblical names are taken from *A Dictionary of Scripture Proper Names* by J.B. Jackson (Neptune, NJ: Loizeaux Brothers, 1909). Common names are taken from *The Name Book* by Dorothea Austin (Minneapolis, MN: Bethany House Publisher, 1982). **Bold print**, *italics*, and CAPITALS are used throughout for clarity of expression and for emphasis. They are sometimes used in the quotation of Scriptures for the same reasons. Comments within brackets [ ] are inserted into many of the Scriptures to clarify and explain their use in relation to the symbols under which they are listed.

Contents

Contents

Preface

The first publication of *Understanding the Dreams You Dream* was barely complete when I began receiving requests for more detailed information on the subject. I immediately began making notes toward a future revision, and happily, at the very first reprint Destiny Image has seen fit to enable me to revise it. It is not surprising that the first edition received such a response; almost everyone who obtains even a little knowledge of this subject immediately desires more. My own intense hunger for an understanding of dream interpretation was awakened when the Lord answered one of my Bible study questions with a dream. After that first experience came an earnest study of God's Word concerning dreams, and from that came a better understanding of how to interpret them. (An account of that first dream and its interpretation can be found in the Introduction.)

From the beginning, I have approached dream interpretation from a biblical standpoint, so I have used both the Bible and my experience as a Christian and minister in the writing of this book. Therefore, at the onset, I would like to clearly state that *every dream is not from God*. The Scriptures declare this: "For a dream cometh through the multitude of business; and a fool's voice is known by multitude of words" (Eccles. 5:3). In this verse a fool's voice is equated to an idle dream, and as we know, God's voice is certainly not that of a fool. Also, there are other Scriptures that speak of dreams in a negative context. This is why I feel that a word of caution is necessary when advising people to pay attention to their dreams.

But, as humans, we tend to err to extremes: We tend to believe either that dreams are just so much nonsense, coming from eating too much, or that all dreams are important and that every symbol has a meaning. Ecclesiastes 5:1-7 is a caution against just such extremes, both in word and in dreams. (My personal experience has been that most dreams are indeed meaningful and helpful, although not all.)

Having said that, I must also quickly add that I have found that *most* dreams *are* from God. As such, they are an accurate reflection of our individual situations. But they are symbolic. Because dreams are symbolic, they appear meaningless. If, in an attempt to understand them an individual tries to consult one or more of the books available on this subject today, he or she will often be left mystified.

The primary obstacle most dreamers must overcome to be able to understand their dreams is symbolism. To solve this problem most authors instruct their readers to meditate on their dreams, which is good advice, yet it is simply not adequate. These authors usually provide the reader with some examples of what their own dreams have meant to them, but even though personal examples are both interesting and informative, they are quite limited in their application.

It is certainly true that through meditation, much can be understood about our dreams; but I have found that when most Christians are told to meditate on their dreams, they do not have the foggiest notion of where to begin. Consequently, I have approached this problem three different ways: specific, detailed directions on how and upon what to meditate; personal examples of dreams from my own experience; and a practical dictionary of symbol definitions.

It has been my experience that it is better to give one's students a place to begin meditating rather than to simply tell them to meditate—hence the symbol dictionary. I have found that a symbol dictionary enables most Christians to begin discerning God's voice immediately. (I have had excellent feedback from readers of the first edition of *Understanding the Dreams You Dream*. In fact, some of the new symbols in this revision are the direct result of some of their questions and comments.)

Additionally, I have attempted to present in this book both normal and the not-so-normal dream situations. To apply only one type of dream interpretation to all dreams is to be as inflexible as restricting each symbol to only one possible definition. For instance, because all dreams are not parables, an attempt to apply parabolic interpretation to a dream that is not a parable is an exercise in futility.

As with the first edition, my primary purpose for writing this book is to guide the reader safely through the complex world of dreams. There are several good books that explain why our Western society has traditionally ignored or rejected the information contained in dreams. I have not, therefore, attempted to cover the history of dreams. (For a background study I recommend: *Dreams: Wisdom Within* by Herman Riffel [Shippensburg, PA: Destiny Image Publishers, 1990].) However, in contrast, there has been little published on the subject of how to interpret dreams from a Christian perspective. Consequently, I have written solely to satisfy this need. It is my prayer that this book will add to your understanding and enjoyment of God's most common method of communication.

Introduction

In 1968 I dreamed a dream that answered a prayer request. I had asked God a question about His Word. In the dream I visited a bus station. While I was there I looked at a travel brochure. The brochure was printed in an unusual way, containing red-letter paragraphs mingled with others in ordinary black print. It was very similar to a red-letter edition Bible.

As I read, I noticed the red-letter paragraphs on the left side of the brochure were the same as the ones on the right side. Then I noticed that the black paragraphs on each side were also identical; that is, each side said the same thing. It was as though the information in the brochure had been printed twice. After noticing this, I awoke.

To me it was just a senseless dream. I idly recounted it to a Christian friend of mine, and his reply startled me. He said, "That dream is from God." When I asked him what it could possibly be intended to tell me, he answered simply, "I don't know."

In response to my conversation with him I prayed and asked God what I had just asked my friend: "God, if this dream is from You, what are You saying to me?" His answer came immediately. Through inspiration, I suddenly understood the meaning.

My original question had been: "God, there are prophets in the New Testament and the Old. Likewise, there are pastors and teachers. But what about apostles? Are they something new just for the New Testament age, or have You had apostles all along?" The answer was profoundly simple. The judges and deliverers of the Old Testament, such as Moses, Joshua, and Samuel, are the same as the apostles and prophets of the New Testament! There is no difference.

After receiving this answer, I realized that I had probably received other answers in the same way, but I had never asked for their meanings. I had simply ignored them. I had treated my dreams like they were junk mail, of no value whatsoever.

Since that day in 1968, I have received many helpful messages from God through dreams. In addition to being helped through my own dreams, I have seen many other people obtain help and comfort by using their dreams as an aid to healing in pastoral counseling.

This book is a condensation of much of what I have learned about interpreting dreams.

Dreams: God's Primary
Means of Communication

God's Communication

For God speaketh once, yea twice, yet man perceiveth it not. In a dream, in a vision of the night, when deep sleep falleth upon men, in slumberings upon the bed; then He openeth the ears of men, and sealeth their instruction. ... Lo, all these things worketh God oftentimes with man (Job 33:14-16,29).

In this Scripture Elihu states that God gives us sealed instructions in the form of dreams. Because these messages are sealed (within parables) we seldom recognize them as being from God. Treating dreams like junk mail, we often throw away the very answers we ask for when we pray for counsel and guidance.

How often do we hear someone say, "I had a weird dream this morning...!" Paul said that God chose the foolish things of the world to confound the wise (see 1 Cor. 1:27). Although many dreams are foolish or senseless to the world, they are precious to those who understand "the hidden wisdom" from above (1 Cor. 2:7).

The way God communicated with people most frequently in the Bible was through dreams. The dreams

3

recorded in the Bible often seem ridiculous, yet their interpretations are quite sensible. For example, Pharaoh dreamed of seven cows that ate seven other cows. Then he dreamed of seven ears of corn that ate seven other ears of corn! The interpretation of these two strange dreams saved Egypt from starvation (see Gen. 41:15-48).

The Bible reveals that in the past God spoke through dreams to saints and sinners alike—warning them, directing them, helping them. He still does. By carefully studying the Bible to find out how God spoke to men in the past we can learn His method of talking to us now.

How often does God communicate with us in dreams? Job 33:29 reveals that God gives us instructions "oftentimes," and Job even says that God visits us every morning! *The postman arrives often, and early:*

> *What is man, that Thou shouldest magnify him? and that Thou shouldest set Thine heart upon him? And that Thou shouldest visit him every morning, and try him every moment?* (Job 7:17-18)

Although night visions (which we will discuss later) are easily recognizable as being from God, dreams are not. The Scriptures state that it is our "old man" that dreams dreams; therefore, they are normally given in parable form. For this reason they must be interpreted if we are to understand what God is saying:

> *And it shall come to pass in the last days, saith God, I will pour out of My Spirit upon all flesh: and your sons and your daughters shall prophesy, and your young men shall see visions, and your old men shall dream dreams* (Acts 2:17).

Interpreting

If there be a messenger with him, an interpreter [of his dreams], *one among a thousand, to show unto man his uprightness: then He is gracious unto him, and saith, Deliver him from going down to the pit: I have found a ransom* (Job 33:23-24).

Although much has been written about dreams, the enormous volume of information concerning dream interpretation found in the Scriptures has been all but ignored! The Bible is filled with dreams and their interpretations. It gives detailed instructions that tell and show us how to interpret them.

The Scriptures were written by the same God who talks to us in dreams. His language has not changed. Our dreams, like those described in the Bible, use word pictures or symbols to convey their concealed messages. Therefore we can study the way symbols are used in Scripture as a guide to the way they are used in our dreams.

Those who attempt to interpret the Scriptures sometimes do so without leaving them in context. When they do this, they often assign meanings to them that the author never intended. Likewise, if the interpretation of a dream is to be accurate, the dream must be left in its setting. The dream and its symbols must be interpreted in light of the life circumstances of the person to whom it is given.

A Snapshot

A dream is like a snapshot, which captures one brief moment out of a lifetime. It cannot be understood fully without knowing something about the life of the person it concerns. Therefore it is not enough to know the meaning of symbols alone. Nevertheless, without an understanding of symbols, we are greatly limited in our ability to navigate through the complex world of dreams.

Even when we are familiar with the background of the person a dream concerns, we should use caution when we apply a symbol's meaning. *Hasty dream interpretations should be avoided.* Even Daniel mulled over Nebuchadnezzar's dream for an hour before he ventured an interpretation, and he knew the king's lifestyle well (see Dan. 4:18-19).

One of the best ways to keep from either simply forgetting about a dream or jumping to conclusions concerning its meaning, is to start a dream journal. Taking the time to write down a dream usually causes one to remember it in greater detail. It also provides a permanent record to come back to.

By recording a dream and what it appears to mean, we can check back later to see if we were correct in our understanding of its meaning. This also appears to be the safest and quickest way to learn to interpret dreams correctly. Sometimes one dream by itself does not provide enough keys to know for certain what God is trying to say. But by comparing several successive dreams, we often find a progressive message unveiled before us. Remember that Job said, "...God speaketh once, yea twice..." (Job 33:14). God is faithful to speak to us again and again if we are really trying to hear what He has to say.

Jesus said to be careful of both *what* you hear, and *how* you hear it (see Mk. 4:24; Lk. 8:18). By listening carefully to what God is saying morning after morning, we are assured of more to come, because He said, "...unto you that hear shall more be given" (Mk. 4:24). Of course the flip side of that is, "...he that hath not, from him shall be taken even that which he hath" (Mk. 4:25).

When recording your dreams, be sure to include each dream's date, your location (home, on vacation, etc.), the feelings that you experienced while dreaming as well as anything important that is going on in your life at the time of the dream. By recording the background information, when you refer back to it later you will still be able to place it into its proper setting.

Dream? Or Night Vision?

There is a difference between a dream and a night vision. A night vision requires little or no interpretation.

In addition to the actual vision seen, a night vision usually has a voice speaking that gives the primary meaning and message of the vision. For example:

> *And a vision appeared to Paul in the night; There stood a man of Macedonia, and prayed him, saying, Come over into Macedonia, and help us. And after he had seen the vision, immediately we endeavored to go into Macedonia, assuredly gathering that the Lord had called us for to preach the gospel unto them* (Acts 16:9-10).

In contrast, a dream seldom lends itself to self-interpretation. *The most common type of dream contains more than one scene; a progressive message unfolds as the dreamer is carried along, either as an observer or as a participant.* Other dreams may contain two or three scenes that all speak a different message, but this is less common. Also, the scene changes in a dream sometimes give different viewpoints of the same subject or express the same idea in different ways rather than reveal a progressive message.

The First Scene

In a dream with more than one scene, *the first scene usually gives the setting*. Like the backdrop of a play, it sets the stage, so that the sealed message it contains can be understood. For example, in the Scripture below, people walking on one another is mentioned before Christ's teaching is given:

> *In the mean time, when there were gathered together an innumerable multitude of people, insomuch that **they trod one upon another**, He began to say unto His disciples first*

of all, Beware ye of the leaven of the Pharisees, which is hypocrisy. For there is nothing covered, that shall not be revealed; neither hid, that shall not be known (Luke 12:1-2).

This stage-setting gives us a parable of the Pharisees' hypocrisy. They trod on the people, oppressing them for their own purposes. They required others to conform to strict laws while they excused themselves from obeying them. Observing this setting makes us aware of emphasis and implications in Christ's words that we would otherwise miss.

In the same way, God usually reveals the subject of His message in the first scene of our dreams. Then, once the subject has been established, the subsequent scenes enlarge upon the plot and carry it forward. This progression can be seen in Daniel's interpretation of Nebuchadnezzar's dream in Daniel 4:20-27:

The tree that thou sawest, which grew, and was strong, whose height reached unto the heaven, and the sight thereof to all the earth; whose leaves were fair, and the fruit thereof much, and in it was meat for all; under which the beasts of the field dwelt, and upon whose branches the fowls of the heaven had their habitation: it is thou, O king, that art grown and become strong: for thy greatness is grown, and reacheth unto heaven, and thy dominion to the end of the earth. And whereas the king saw a watcher and an holy one coming down from heaven, and saying, Hew the tree down, and destroy it; yet leave the stump of the roots thereof in the earth, even with a band of iron and brass, in the tender grass of the field; and let it be wet with the dew of heaven, and let his portion be with the beasts of the field, till seven times pass over him; this is the interpretation, O king, and this is the decree of the most High, which is come upon my Lord the king: that they shall drive thee from men, and thy dwelling shall be with the beasts of the field, and they shall make thee to eat grass as oxen, and they shall wet thee with the dew of heaven, and seven times shall pass over thee, till thou know that the most High ruleth in the kingdom of men, and giveth it to whomsoever He will. And whereas they commanded to leave the stump of the tree roots; thy kingdom shall be sure unto thee, after that thou shalt have known that the heavens do rule. Wherefore, O king, let my counsel be acceptable unto thee, and break off thy sins by righteousness, and thine iniquities by showing mercy to the poor; if it may be a lengthening of thy tranquility.

Notice that this dream has two scenes. The first scene establishes that the dream is about the growth and prosperity of King Nebuchadnezzar and his kingdom. The second scene reveals God's displeasure with the king's prideful conduct and foretells of certain chastisement to come.

Because dreams can cover several different subjects and areas of our lives, it is important to correctly discern the subject matter to which the dream refers if we are to utilize the message properly. If we don't do this, we may easily apply a dream to the wrong area of our lives, or even incorrectly apply it to another person when God is really speaking to us about ourselves.

This is especially true when a dream contains people we can identify. Friends and family members are often used as symbols. Sometimes they represent ourselves; sometimes they represent another friend or family member; and sometimes they simply represent themselves. Only careful attention to all the scenes and symbols used in a dream will keep us from making this type of misapplication.

Application Aids Interpretation

Without proper application, correct interpretation is difficult, if not impossible. To determine what a dream is about, and apply the message correctly, first ask yourself these two questions: "*Who* does this dream refer to?" and "*What* is it really about?" Then, examine the action in the dream to determine the message. In other words, what is the dream's setting? What are the people saying and doing?

To answer the first question, always examine yourself to see if the dream can apply directly to yourself. A dream is usually both for and about the one who dreams it. Because we do not know our own heart, God uses dreams to reveal its deep, dark secrets to us. The problem is, we really don't want to know the secrets of our hearts! So, God often has to use other people to represent different aspects of ourselves. These people may be strangers, family and friends, or just acquaintances. There may be just one person, or there may be several; they may be dead or alive, former friends, or distant relatives. But their words and actions will reveal hidden virtues, faults, or sins about ourselves that we are simply ignoring or have completely justified.

When answering the second question (what the dream is about) remember that God's ultimate desire is that we should walk in righteousness. As the preceding dream about Nebuchadnezzar shows, many of our dreams are about our personal conduct or holiness. Another area of our lives that God often communicates with us about in dreams is our livelihood. As John wrote in Third John 1:2, God desires above all things that we may prosper and be in health, even as our soul prospers. Therefore God speaks to us concerning our relationship with Him, our jobs, our health, and our relationships with others.

For example, I once dreamed that I was having a blood test done. I could see my blood as though I was looking through the microscope along with the laboratory technician. My blood had large, irregular, red cells with the word *meat* written on them. When I awoke I knew that God was warning me that my cholesterol level was getting too high from eating too much meat.

Another significant dream was one that my wife had. We had a small service business, and unbeknownst to us our service manager decided to go in business for himself at our expense. My wife dreamed that he was in my office wearing a face mask like the one worn by the Lone Ranger, and he was stealing papers. She told me the dream, and when I went to the office and checked, I discovered that a card file containing all our customers' names and addresses was missing. Acting on the information in the dream, I immediately went to his house and recovered them. In doing so I saved our business from considerable loss.

It is not uncommon for God to give a pastor or traveling minister a sermon topic or message in a dream. He may also show him a problem in the church that needs to be dealt with. Although the subject matter of dreams is almost endless, that which concerns us concerns God, and He is faithful to communicate with us when we diligently seek Him for His guidance.

Once we know the particular subject God is talking about and who He is referring to, proper dream interpretation is usually not difficult. But if these two things are not determined correctly, any interpretation we may venture will be misguided or incorrect.

Checking the Source

On the other hand, not every dream we have is from God. How can we tell the difference? When we learn to communicate with God by speaking to Him in prayer and hearing His reply, we soon learn that everything we hear is not His voice. Instead, God simply inserts a thought into our thoughts, often answering our questions when we are not even thinking about what we have asked.

Sometimes we receive God's thoughts in dreams the same way. We may be idly dreaming a rambling, almost incoherent dream, and God will insert a clear, meaningful message into it. Trying to remember our rambling dream is not practical, often not possible, and certainly not necessary. The portion containing God's message will be remembered if we faithfully try to do so. Sometimes we have no choice but to simply forget the rest:

> *But the Comforter, which is the Holy Ghost, whom the Father will send in My name, He shall teach you all things, and bring all things to your remembrance, whatsoever I have said unto you* (John 14:26).

As a general rule, if after substituting the symbols in a dream with the key words or thoughts they symbolize, one still finds no recognizable message, then the dream is probably just junk mail, proceeding from somewhere in the confused or troubled regions of the soul. It is not from God. (It should still be recorded, however, for later examination in relation to other subsequent dreams may reveal that its meaning was simply not apparent at the time it was received.)

This is not to say that unless a dream is directly from God that it is not useful. Our dreams reveal the secrets of our hearts (even when we really don't want to know them). The Bible says that it is our spirit that truly knows us, not our conscious mind (see 1 Cor. 2:11). Although there are times when our spirit will cry out for help to us in the night, these messages can be understood using the same method and keys used with other dreams.

Because some of our dreams are not from God, we should exercise reasonable caution when we apply them. We should observe the same basic precautions with dreams that we apply to other sources of personal guidance. Information and instructions obtained from dreams should be confirmed in other ways before we act upon them.

For instance, a strong obsession for something may cause one to dream of obtaining it (see Jer. 29:8)! This happened to me once when I was attempting to sell a business that I owned. It had become a real burden to me, and I was anxious to sell it. One night I dreamed that a man came and paid me in cash the exact amount that I was asking for! He never came, and it's good that he didn't. I finally realized there were other ways besides selling it to unload some of the burden. Later, it became a real blessing to me.

God's timing is another factor that must be taken into consideration when we are working out His will in our lives. Sometimes He tells us what He will do for us, but we have to wait for Him to do it. Joseph is a good example of this. He was 17 years old when he had the two prophetic dreams recorded in the Bible. However, he was 30 years old before they came to pass (see Gen. 37:2,5; 41:46). The Bible states, "Until the time that his word came: the word of the Lord tried him" (Psalm 105:19).

Although 13 years may be longer than most of us want to wait before our dreams are fulfilled, sometimes we really don't have a choice. If we try to rush things by taking them into our own hands, we usually wind up with an Ishmael in our lives (see Gen. 21:11). It is much wiser to obtain confirmation from other sources before we take action based on directions received in dreams:

...In the mouth of two or three witnesses shall every word be established (2 Corinthians 13:1).

Conversely, sometimes a dream simply confirms instructions that one has already received from a different source. God's dealing with Gideon is a good example of this:

And it came to pass the same night, that the Lord said unto [Gideon], Arise, get thee down unto the host; for I have delivered it into thine hand. But if thou fear to go down, go thou with Phurah thy servant down to the host: and thou shalt hear what they say; and afterward shall thine hands be strengthened to go down unto the host. Then went he down with Phurah his servant unto the outside of the armed men that were in the host. And the Midianites and the Amalekites and all the children of the east lay along in the valley like grasshoppers for multitude; and their camels were without number, as the sand by the sea side for multitude. And when Gideon was come, behold, there was a man that told a dream unto his fellow, and said, Behold, I dreamed a dream, and, lo, a cake of barley bread tumbled into the host of Midian, and came unto a tent, and smote it that it fell, and overturned it, that the tent lay along. And his fellow answered and said, This is nothing else save the sword of Gideon the son of Joash, a man of Israel: for into his hand hath God delivered Midian, and all the host. And it was so, when Gideon heard the telling of the dream, and the interpretation thereof, that he worshipped, and returned into the host of Israel, and said, Arise; for the Lord hath delivered into your hand the host of Midian (Judges 7:9-15).

The power of this type of confirmation is seen in Gideon's reaction to this dream. An angel had visited him and commissioned him to deliver Israel. Then he supernaturally confirmed the commission. After the angel's visitation God responded to Gideon's prayer and manipulated the dew both on the ground and on a fleece that Gideon placed out for additional confirmation. But it wasn't until Gideon heard his victory declared in a dream that he was bold enough to act upon God's command and go to war (see Judg. 6:11-22,36-40).

There is one obvious way of checking a dream to see if it is from God. *God's messages are always consistent with His written Word.* A dream may seem like a fable, or even include wrong or sinful actions, but when properly interpreted the message it contains will always be in accordance with the righteous principles of the Bible. Like some of the stories in the Bible, the dream content may *appear* very negative, yet contain beautiful, positive truth. A dream from God will never instruct us to do something evil. Like the Word itself, a dream from God will equip us to walk in truth and righteousness:

> *All scripture is given by inspiration of God, and* [every dream that is from God] *is profitable for doctrine, for reproof, for correction, for instruction in righteousness: that the man of God may be perfect, thoroughly furnished unto all good works* (2 Timothy 3:16-17).

R- and X-Rated Dreams

Understanding sexually explicit and violent dreams is especially helpful for enabling us to walk in righteousness. Dreaming of an illicit, intimate sexual encounter often reveals the need of deliverance from a spirit of lust (see Mt. 10:8). Although adultery and fornication are works of the flesh, it is abnormal to have sexually explicit dreams unless one is influenced by an unclean spirit. Such a spirit often makes his presence known by taking advantage of a person's unconscious state (sleep) to act out his desires in that person's dreams (see 2 Cor. 11:4).

Likewise, a terrifying dream of being stabbed or killed often reveals the presence of a spirit of fear from which one needs deliverance (see 2 Tim. 1:7; Heb. 2:14-15). (I have personally known of Christians who were literally tormented by bad dreams until they were delivered through prayer.) The very word used to describe such a dream, *nightmare*, means a dream given by a monster or demon.

Dreaming of personally hurting or killing someone can alert us to the presence of a spirit of jealousy or hate lurking somewhere beneath our consciousness (see Prov. 6:34; 1 Jn. 3:15). Our unconscious rage or desire for revenge will be revealed by the violent behavior in the dream. James tells us that emotions like these come straight from the devil:

> *But if ye have bitter envying and strife in your hearts, glory not, and lie not against the truth* [deceiving ourselves]. *This wisdom descendeth not from above, but is earthly, sensual, devilish* (James 3:14-15).

In R- and X-rated dreams, *sometimes* the individual symbols do not reveal anything specific within themselves; rather the *feelings* of lust, rage, hatred, or overwhelming fear give us the information we need to understand the significance of the dream. I stress *sometimes* because there is another type of "nightmare" that everyone should be aware of, and in these dreams, the symbols *are* important. These terrifying dreams come straight from God! Job complained about having this type of dream in Job 7:13-14.

> When I say, My bed shall comfort me, my couch shall ease my complaint; then Thou scarest me with dreams, and terrifiest me through visions (Job 7:13-14).

In these dreams, the symbols are significant, but concentrating on them can sometimes cause one to overlook the main point. Like the man who "couldn't see the forest for the trees," focusing on the symbols in this type of dream may add confusion instead of bringing clarification. The best way to illustrate this is with an actual dream I encountered several years ago. (I provide this account with the full permission of the dreamer. Some details have been left out due to space limitations.) Instead of trying to identify the symbols and interpret them, first pay attention to the action of the dream.

This dreamer started her letter by saying, "Ordinarily, I don't have nightmares, the kind where you wake up in the middle of the night frozen with fear as if it really was happening, but I did the other night... If this was something from the Lord to minister a message to me, I don't know how to pray concerning this...

"I dreamed I was standing in my bedroom by a window ironing when a blonde-haired woman (seemingly a neighbor, but I didn't know her) came in for help. She wanted to use our phone to call for help. After dialing she said, 'I keep trying to call out on your line but I keep getting a busy signal.' I told her we didn't have our phone hooked up yet. She said she was trying to get away from someone. About that time I looked out the window and saw the man that she was running from coming toward the house... When I saw him coming I could tell that he was angry. (At this point the woman disappeared from the dream.) The man got in through the back door...

"The man grabbed me by the arm at knife point and began to drag me out the front door to a neighbor's house... The man was dragging me up the steps with him and was banging on their front door. They hesitated, but finally opened the door... At this time I broke free and began to run. The angry man cursed at me and swore he would kill me. I ran back to my house through the front door. I realized I had to get help so I jumped out the back door, and I began running down a blacktopped highway. I saw houses and lights ahead...

"Finally, after having a hard time deciding what house to go to for help, I ran up to a trailer house with a car parked in the driveway. As I ran up the steps I saw that the door was a double glass sliding door. I saw a man standing at a desk talking on the phone. He motioned for me to come in. I went in and told him that I needed help, that a man was after me. I walked into an adjoining room to wait for him to get through with his telephone conversation, but I overheard him laugh and say to the other party, 'Man, this is your lucky day—the woman that escaped from you just came up here for help!' I ran out the back door, trying again to figure out where to go and ask for help... [after another episode similar to those above, the woman ended the account of her dream with] ...I was so scared! I woke up frozen in a state of fear."

When I received the letter telling of this dream I contacted the woman and told her the dream seemed to be saying that she was under a perpetual curse. (Regardless of where she ran, every time she escaped, the evil man was able to find her and put her back in danger.) This action speaks of a permanent curse. The Scripture I gave her to read was Amos 5:19: "As if a man did flee from a lion, and a bear met him; or went into the house, and leaned his hand on the wall, and a serpent bit him." The primary symbol of her dream was the "back" door. A back door usually means the past. I told her that the dream appeared to be telling her that her present distress was coming directly from her past. Later, through counseling, she discovered that the curse came from an earlier period in her life when she had participated in the occult. When she asked God's forgiveness and renounced her involvement with the occult, her entire life changed dramatically.

In this dream the evil man's actions revealed her problem. The back door revealed the source of both her problem and the answer to it. The man came *in* through the back door, and each time she escaped she ran *out* the back door to find help! Like Job, who said, "For Thou writest bitter things against me, and makest me to possess the iniquities of my youth" (Job 13:26), it was not until she dealt with her past that she was set free. Although there are several more significant symbols in this dream, like the telephone that is not hooked up (ineffective prayer) and the trailer house (temporary refuge), they add nothing to the initial interpretation of the dream. Once she repented and was set free from the curse, her prayer life blossomed and her financial situation turned around beautifully. As Jesus said, once she knew the truth, the truth made her free (see Jn. 8:32).

Emotions in Dreams

As we have seen, our emotions (*as they are felt while we are dreaming*) are significant. The emotional response to the message after we wake up can be misleading. For example, if we dream of a person's death and in the dream we are at peace, or even rejoicing, it does not follow that God is saying that person will die. In fact, if the person is lost, dreaming of his death may foretell of his repentance and consequential salvation. Although such a dream would trouble us upon waking, the key to understanding what a dream is saying is always found in the emotions we feel *while* we are dreaming.

Colors Are Important

Come now, and let us reason together, saith the Lord: though your sins be as scarlet, they shall be as white as snow;

though they be red like crimson, they shall be as wool (Isaiah 1:18).

Although most of our dreams are in black and white, sometimes certain colored objects appear in them. *Colors are symbolic, supplying additional information about the objects that are colored.* For example, if you previously owned a blue car of a certain model and you dream of owning and driving that same car, God is probably talking to you about your past. The blue car represents an earlier period of your life (although not necessarily the exact time when you owned the car).

On the other hand, if you dream you are driving a blue car that is yours, but in real life you have never owned such a car, then the color has a different meaning. In the first example the color blue simply identified the car as something that is part of your past. In the second example, the color blue is referring to the spiritual aspects of your present life or ministry (see BLUE and AUTOMOBILE in the Key Word Dictionary).

Literal or Symbolic?

Another common problem in solving the riddles offered to us by dreams is that of discerning when a dream is symbolic (a parable) and when it is literal. *As a general rule, if a dream can be taken literally, it should be.* If there is something in a dream that is not literal, however, then the entire dream should be interpreted as if the objects, and sometimes even the people it contains, are symbols.

For instance, in the above example concerning the two blue cars, neither dream can be taken literally. In the first example, you no longer own the car. Therefore you cannot be driving it as your own. In the second example, you have never owned such a car, so again the dream must be symbolic.

However, if you dream you are driving the car you really own, to the job you presently have, and that you are involved in an accident on the street on which you actually work, then you should pray for God to prevent this from happening to you and drive carefully!

There will normally be a key—a clue—something in each dream that will reveal whether it is literal or symbolic. As a rule, if there is an object or person in a dream that cannot be taken literally, then the entire dream should be viewed as symbolic or as a parable. However, if everything in a dream is as it actually is in real life, the dream is usually literal.

For instance, I once dreamed that my brother called me and asked if I was interested in renting a house that his employer had for rent. I said that I was, and in the dream I went and examined the house. It was a light-colored brick. Inside, the floor was littered with trash. I noticed that quite a lot of money was scattered among the trash.

After I awoke I was still meditating on the dream when my phone rang. It was my brother calling. He asked me the same question he had asked in the dream, "Are you interested in renting a different house?" I

replied, "Yes, I've been praying for a better place."
When I actually saw the house, it was identical to the
one in the dream, trash and all. I rented it. And in addition to the money that was scattered on the floor, the
landlord gave us half the first month's rent for cleaning
it. (Two biblical examples of literal dreams are found in
Genesis 20:3-7 and First Kings 3:5-15.)

Changeable or Unchangeable?

Regardless of whether a dream is literal or a parable,
there are several scriptural examples that show us that,
when necessary, we can change the outcome from that
in the dream. The situation a dream reveals or foretells
can usually be changed through prayer:

> *Thus hath the Lord God shown unto me; and, behold, He
> formed grasshoppers in the beginning of the shooting up of
> the latter growth; and, lo, it was the latter growth after the
> king's mowings. And it came to pass, that when they had
> made an end of eating the grass of the land* [in the dream
> or vision], *then I said, O Lord God, forgive, I beseech Thee:
> by whom shall Jacob arise? for he is small. The Lord re-
> pented for this: It shall not be, saith the Lord. Thus hath the
> Lord God shown unto me: and, behold, the Lord God called
> to contend by fire, and it devoured the great deep, and did
> eat up a part. Then said I, O Lord God, cease, I beseech
> Thee: by whom shall Jacob arise? for he is small. The Lord
> repented for this: This also shall not be, saith the Lord God*
> (Amos 7:1-6).

One can see from the example quoted above that
Amos' intercession changed God's mind concerning

destroying the nation of Israel. Like the prophecy given by Jonah against Nineveh, dreams often warn of impending trouble or danger. These warnings are given so that we can pray and, when necessary, repent. *Prayer changes things!*

Repetitious Dreams

Sometimes as we meditate on a dream we realize that we have dreamed the same thing before. The second dream may not always use the same objects or people, yet the same hidden message is apparent. An example of this is found in the two dreams of Pharaoh mentioned in the preceding chapter. In the first dream, seven cows ate seven other cows. In the second, seven ears of corn ate seven other ears of corn. The two dreams use different symbols, yet obviously contain the same message.

Joseph declared that the repetition of the message meant it was established of God. In other words, it would certainly happen! From this we can see that repetitious dreams are especially important.

And Joseph said unto Pharaoh, The dream of Pharaoh is one: God hath shown Pharaoh what He is about to do. ... And for that the dream was doubled unto Pharaoh twice; it is because the thing is established by God, and God will shortly bring it to pass (Genesis 41:25,32).

Shortly before going into full time ministry I had these two dreams: In the first, I was driving a school bus across a river, and the bridge I was on suddenly came to an end! As I sailed off the end I was gripped with fear. As I fell, I found myself hoping that the water wasn't too deep so that maybe I could drive out.

A few months later I dreamed that I was teaching a class about prophetic ministry. After the session was over, I was driving across the top of a very high building when I suddenly drove off the edge! As I fearfully plunged downward I thought, *I have a parachute to keep me from falling too hard.*

The fulfillment came about three months later. I was suddenly thrust into full-time ministry and had to completely trust God for my income. Although I was "fearful" at first, I soon realized that God was well able to supply my needs, even without a "regular" salary.

Understanding Symbolic Dreams (Parables)

All these things spake Jesus unto the multitude in parables; and without a parable spake He not unto them (Matthew 13:34).

Jesus gave an example for understanding symbols in the parable of the sower. Because most dreams are parables, the method He used to decipher this parable is also the proper way to unravel the mystery of dreams. Because Jesus said that the parable of the sower explains the way to interpret *all* parables, I have quoted it in its entirety:

Hearken; Behold, there went out a sower to sow: and it came to pass, as he sowed, some fell by the way side, and the fowls of the air came and devoured it up. And some fell on stony ground, where it had not much earth; and immediately it *sprang up, because it had no depth of earth: but when the sun was up, it was scorched; and because it had no root, it withered away. And some fell among thorns, and the thorns grew up, and choked it, and it yielded no fruit. And other fell on good ground, and did yield fruit that sprang up and increased; and brought forth, some thirty, and some sixty, and some an hundred. And He said unto them, He that hath ears to hear, let him hear. And when He was alone, they that were about Him with the twelve asked of Him the parable. And He said unto them, Unto you it is given to know the mystery of the kingdom of God: but unto them that are without, all these things are done in parables: that seeing they may see, and not perceive; and hearing they may hear, and not understand; lest at any time they should be converted, and their sins should be forgiven them. **And He said unto them, Know ye not this parable? and how then will ye know all parables?*** (Mark 4:3-13)

By comparing the thoughts obtained from the Key Word Dictionary with Jesus' interpretation, one can see that He simply replaced each symbol in the parable with its respective meaning. Usually one word, or the thought contained in that word, was sufficient to give them the understanding He wanted them to have. I have inserted some additional symbol meanings into the text to help clarify the parable.

The sower [preacher] *soweth* [preaches] *the word* [seed]. *And these are they by the way side* [path of willful un-righteousness]*, where the word is sown; but when they have heard, Satan* [the fowls] *cometh immediately, and taketh away the word that was sown in their hearts. And these are they likewise which are sown on stony ground* [hard hearts]; *who, when they have heard the word, immediately receive it with gladness* [the joy of salvation]; *and have no root* [conviction or steadfastness] *in themselves, and so endure but for a time: afterward, when affliction* [trouble] *or persecution* [opposition, rejection, etc.] *ariseth for the word's sake, immediately they are offended. And these are they which are sown among thorns* [debts, natural responsibilities, etc.]; *such as hear the word, and the cares of this world, and the deceitfulness of riches, and the lusts of other things entering in, choke the word* [hinder its fulfillment or performance], *and it becometh unfruitful. And these are they which are sown on good ground; such as hear the word, and receive it, and bring forth fruit, some thirtyfold, some sixty, and some an hundred* (Mark 4:14-20).

To further expand this parable let us use the keys obtained from the section of the Key Word Dictionary entitled "Numbers." When we do this we can see that 30-fold means *conformed* (and therefore accepted), 60 means *image*, and 100 means *fullness*, or in this case, *full measure*. Therefore we can paraphrase the last sentence of the above verse in this way:

"And these are they which are sown on good ground; such as hear the word, and receive it, and bring forth fruit because they are conformed to His image and likeness. For this reason they are abundantly fruitful."

Compare this paraphrased interpretation to the Scriptures below:

*For whom He did foreknow, He also did predestinate **to be conformed to the image of His Son**, that He might be the firstborn among many brethren* (Romans 8:29).

*Till we all come in the unity of the faith, and of the knowl-
edge of the Son of God, unto a perfect man, **unto the measure of the stature of the fulness of Christ** (Ephesians
4:13).*

*If ye abide in Me, and My words abide in you, ye shall ask
what ye will, and it shall be done unto you. **Herein is My
Father glorified, that ye bear much fruit;** so shall ye be
My disciples* (John 15:7-8).

Another example of this method of dream interpretation is found in the Book of Daniel. The Bible states
that Daniel had understanding in all dreams and visions
(see Dan. 1:17). In Daniel 2:31-45 and in Daniel 4:10-27,
we find that Daniel, who was an authority in dreams,
used exactly the same method of interpretation illus-
trated above when he explained the meaning of Nebuchadnezzar's dreams. He simply replaced the symbols
with the key words or thoughts that the symbols repre-
sented to decipher the messages contained in the
dreams.

To illustrate this method, let's consider the symbols
in the two repetitious dreams I referred to earlier—
where I drove suddenly off both a bridge and a tall
building. The school bus in the first dream referred to
my teaching ministry. The bridge was my support. My
income suddenly came to an end, and I was thrust into
full-time ministry. The broken bridge and falling both
refer to loss of support. In the second dream, I was ministering and suddenly found myself falling off a building, but was supported by a parachute, which in turn is
supported by air. Air represents spirit. Through this

God was saying that even though my weekly salary would suddenly come to an end, He would sustain me.

Positive or Negative, Good or Bad?

Symbols, like most words, can be used both positively and negatively. For instance, when we use the word *cool*, we may be referring to something good or bad. "The soup is cool" may mean that the soup is cool enough to eat or that it needs to be reheated. "This room certainly is cool" may mean that the heat needs to be turned up or that the temperature feels good (to someone who has just came in from the summer heat). Additionally, to say that someone is cool may mean that that person is not friendly or that he or she needs a jacket. It may even indicate admiration because the person "has it all together."

Likewise, almost all symbols can have both positive (good) and negative (bad) meanings. The following scriptural example uses each of two metals, brass and iron, as a symbol with two different, though related, meanings.

> *For brass* [the letter of the law] *I will bring gold* [wisdom], *and for iron* [bondage] *I will bring silver* [knowledge or redemption], *and for wood* [works of the flesh] *brass* [God's grace or truth], *and for stones* [accusations witnessing against you] *iron* [strength or justification]: *I will also make thy officers peace, and thine exacters righteousness* (Isaiah 60:17).

Initially brass is used to symbolize the Law of Moses, then it is employed to symbolize God's Word of grace and truth. The bondage of the law is symbolized by iron, which then comes to represent the power of the Holy Spirit given to Christians who are justified through Christ.

In this next Scripture notice how the symbol for people (trees) is used both positively and negatively (both in a good and a bad sense):

> *And all the trees* [people] *of the field* [world] *shall know that I the Lord have brought down the high tree* [haughty person], *have exalted the low tree* [humble person], *have dried up the green tree* [carnal person], *and have made the dry tree* [repented person, dead with Christ] *to flourish...* (Ezekiel 17:24).

The most important thing to remember about interpreting symbols is, *never be narrow-minded*. Symbols, like words, are very flexible. When one knows the context of a dream and the circumstances of the dreamer's life, one can properly assign the right meanings. Without this knowledge one can only guess.

For instance, it is possible for an ant in a dream to mean several different things. One meaning comes directly from the Bible. Others come from our personal experience. In the Key Word Dictionary I have listed several possible meanings. These include the following: *industrious*: wise; diligent; prepared for the future; nuisance; stinging or angry words. The context of the dream must determine which meaning to use in your interpretation.

When one dreams of ants at a picnic, the context would obviously lean toward "nuisance" as the meaning of the symbol, even though it is their industrious nature that makes them such a nuisance! To dream of ants gathering food would relate directly to the key word definition of industrious, diligent preparation for the future. Likewise, dreaming of being bit or stung by ants would fit the "stinging or angry words" definition.

Sometimes a symbol has a meaning to one person that would not fit another. The example of the blue car, which we used earlier, could only mean the past to someone who had previously owned such a car. Another example is a pet dog. A dog is usually a symbol for an unclean spirit or attitude—such as strife or contention. But dreaming about your own pet dog, which you love, would normally symbolize something good, something close to you that you cherish, not something bad.

When we are trying to determine the object and subject of a dream, we ask ourselves the questions, "*Who* does this dream refer to?" and "*What* is it really about?" Likewise, when we are trying to decipher a symbol, the first question we should ask is, "What does this symbol mean to *me*?" Like the pet dog previously mentioned, only the pet's owner would recognize its correct meaning when used as a symbol in his dream.

I encountered an interesting example of this once when I was helping a lady pastor interpret a dream. In this dream two angels came to her house and told her not to worry about YWAM (Youth With A Mission), that every need they had would be met. Although she had previously told me that her church was having financial difficulty, I could not see how God supplying a mission organization's needs had anything to do with her situation. Then she said, "We jokingly say that 'YWAM' means, 'Youth Without Any Money,' because they have to do so much with so little." It was not until then that I realized that God was simply using her personal perception of YWAM (doing God's work without any money) to assure her that He would meet all her own needs.

God will use names that rhyme, puns, riddles, proverbs, almost anything imaginable to hide the truth from our "old man" when He speaks to us in the night. God, who created the heavens and the earth and all things therein, has boundless imagination. If we are going to keep up with Him, we must stretch ours. He used the stars to represent Abraham's descendants, the sun to characterize Himself, the moon to portray the Church, lambs to illustrate His little children, and wolves to describe their enemies! He can and will use almost anything to get His point across.

He will speak to a plumber using pipe wrenches and dope, stopped-up drains and fireplugs; but He will employ completely different symbols when He talks to a doctor or lawyer. Yet, there are objects that are common to everyone, and God uses these to speak to each of us at one time or another. Many of these common symbols (such as objects, actions, people, places, etc.) are listed and expanded on in the Key Word Dictionary that follows.

A Key Word Dictionary
of Dream Symbols
With Scriptural Illustrations

Animals/Birds/Fish/Insects

ALLIGATOR (or Crocodile)—*Ancient:* (*Note:* Alligators are Old World animals.) Evil out of the past (through inheritance or personal sin); danger; destruction; evil spirit. (See BEAR.)

Canst thou draw out leviathan [a crocodile] *with an hook? or his tongue with a cord which thou lettest down? ... None is so fierce that dare stir him up: who then is able to stand before Me?* (Job 41:1,10)

ANT—*Industrious:* Wise; diligent; prepared for the future; nuisance; stinging or angry words.

Go to the ant, thou sluggard; consider her ways, and be wise: which having no guide, overseer, or ruler, provideth her meat in the summer, and gathereth her food in the harvest (Proverbs 6:6-8).

He that gathereth in summer [like the ant] *is a wise son: but he that sleepeth in harvest is a son that causeth shame* (Proverbs 10:5).

BAT—*Witchcraft:* (*Note:* A bat is a creature of the night.) Flighty; unstable; fear (as in "deathly afraid of bats").

And these are they which ye shall have in abomination among the fowls; they shall not be eaten, they are an abomination...the bat (Leviticus 11:13-19).

BEAR—*Destroyer:* Destruction; an evil curse (through inheritance or personal sin, including financial lost or hardship); economic loss (as in "a bear market"); danger; opposition; Russia. (See SNAKE.)

As if a man did flee from a lion, and a bear met him; or went into the house, and leaned his hand on the wall, and a serpent bit him (Amos 5:19).

And [Elisha] *went up from thence unto Bethel: and as he was going up by the way, there came forth little children out of the city, and mocked him...And he turned back, and looked on them, and cursed them in the name of the Lord. And there came forth two she bears out of the wood, and tare forty and two children of them* (2 Kings 2:23-24).

BEAVER—*Industrious:* Busy (as in "busy as a beaver"); diligent; clever; ingenious.

He becometh poor that dealeth with a slack hand: but the hand of the diligent maketh rich (Proverbs 10:4).

Through wisdom is an house builded; and by understanding it is established (Proverbs 24:3).

BEES—*Chastisement or Offense:* Stinging words; affliction; busybody; busy (as in "busy as a bee"); gossip. (See HORNETS.)

And the Amorites, which dwelt in that mountain, came out against you, and chased [chastised] *you, as bees do, and destroyed you in Seir, even unto Hormah* (Deuteronomy 1:44).

They compassed me about like bees; they are quenched as the fire of thorns: for in the name of the Lord I will destroy them (Psalm 118:12).

And withal they learn to be idle, wandering [or buzzing] *about from house to house; and not only idle, but tattlers also and busybodies, speaking things which they ought not* (1 Timothy 5:13).

BIRD—*Spirit:* Holy Spirit; demon; man; gossip; message. (See CROW/RAVEN, EAGLE, OWL, VULTURE, etc.)

And John bare record, saying, I saw the Spirit descending from heaven like a dove, and it abode upon Him (John 1:32).

Curse not the king, no not in thy thought; and curse not the rich in thy bedchamber: for a bird of the air shall carry the voice, and that which hath wings shall tell the matter (Ecclesiastes 10:20).

And he cried mightily with a strong voice, saying, Babylon the great is fallen, is fallen, and is become the habitation of devils, and the hold of every foul spirit, and a cage of every unclean and hateful bird (Revelation 18:2).

BULL—*Persecution:* Spiritual warfare; opposition; accusation; slander; threat; economic increase (as in "a bull market"). (See CALF.)

Many bulls have compassed me: strong bulls of Bashan have beset me round (Psalm 22:12).

BUTTERFLY—*Freedom:* Flighty (flitting about); fragile; temporary glory. **Cocoon** = *Metamorphosis;* transformation; change. **Caterpillar** = *Devourer;* potential.

And be not conformed to this world: but be ye transformed by the renewing of your mind... (Romans 12:2).

...and that which the cankerworm hath left hath the caterpillar eaten (Joel 1:4).

BUZZARD—See VULTURE.

CALF—*Increase:* Prosperity; idolatry; false worship; stubbornness; children of the Kingdom. **Cow or Heifer** = *a rebellious woman.*

The inhabitants of Samaria [mixed, incorrect worship] *shall fear because of the calves* [idolatry, i.e., materialism, as seen in the popular prosperity doctrine] *of Bethaven* [house of vanity; i.e., as opposed to Bethel, the house of God]: *for the people thereof shall mourn over it, and the priests thereof that rejoiced on it, for the glory thereof, because it is departed from it* [see Jer. 7:8-11] (Hosea 10:5).

But unto you that fear My name shall the Sun of righteousness arise with healing in His wings; and ye shall go forth, and grow up as calves of the stall (Malachi 4:2).

For Israel slideth back as a [stubborn] *backsliding heifer* (Hosea 4:16a).

And he received them [gold earrings] *at their hand, and fashioned it with a graving tool, after he had made it a molten calf* [idol, i.e., covetousness (see Col. 3:5)]: *and they said, These be thy gods, O Israel, which brought thee up out of the land of Egypt. ... And the Lord plagued the people, because they made the calf, which Aaron* [their priest, or preacher] *made* (Exodus 32:4,35).

CAMEL—*Endurance (because of their ability to go for long periods without water):* Long journey; ungainly (not graceful).

And so, after he had patiently endured, he obtained the promise (Hebrews 6:15).

CAT—*Self-willed:* Not trainable (unteachable spirit); predator; unclean spirit; bewitching charm (witchcraft); stealthy; sneaky; crafty; deception; self-pity. **Personal Pet** = *Something precious.*

And, behold, there met him a woman with the attire of an harlot, and subtle of heart. (She is loud and stubborn; her feet abide not in her house: now is she without, now in the streets [ally cat], *and lieth in wait at every corner.) ... With her much fair speech she caused him to yield, with the flattering of her lips* [purring] *she forced him* (Proverbs 7:10-12,21).

CHICKEN—*Fear:* Cowardliness. **Hen** = *Protection;* gossip. **Rooster** = *Boasting;* bragging; proud. **Chick** = *Defenseless;* innocent.

Then I said unto you, Dread not, neither be afraid of them (Deuteronomy 1:29).

O Jerusalem, Jerusalem, which killest the prophets, and stonest them that are sent unto thee; how often would I have gathered thy children together, as a hen doth gather her brood under her wings, and ye would not! (Luke 13:34)

And he said unto Him, Lord, I am ready to go with Thee, both into prison, and to death. And He said, I tell thee, Peter, the cock [rooster] *shall not crow this day, before that thou shalt thrice deny that thou knowest Me* [John 18:27 reads: "Peter then denied again: and immediately the cock crew" (reminding Peter of his empty boast).] (Luke 22:33-34).

COW—See CALF.

CRAWFISH—*Retreat:* Coward. **With Raised Claws** = *Defensive;* cautious; renege on a promise (as in "he got cold feet and crawfished out of the deal").

And all the men of Israel, when they saw the man [Goliath], *fled from him, and were sore afraid* (1 Samuel 17:24).

CROW/RAVEN—*Confusion:* Outspoken person, usually operating under the influence of a spirit of envy or strife (which causes confusion and disorder); hateful; direct path (straight line, as in "as the crow flies"); God's minister of justice or provision.

For where envying and strife is, there is confusion and every evil work (James 3:16).

...The raven shall dwell in it: and He shall stretch out upon it the line of confusion, and the stones of emptiness (Isaiah 34:11).

Let them be ashamed and brought to confusion together that rejoice at mine hurt: let them be clothed with shame and dishonor that magnify themselves [and speak] *against me* (Psalm 35:26).

The eye that mocketh at his father, and despiseth to obey his mother, the ravens of the valley [depression; grief; confusion, etc.] *shall pick it out...* (Proverbs 30:17).

I have commanded the ravens to feed thee there. ... And the ravens brought him bread and flesh in the morning, and bread and flesh in the evening... (1 Kings 17:4b,6).

DEER—*Graceful:* Swift; sure-footed; agile; timid. **Buck** = *Regal;* rule. **Antlers** = *Power;* authority. (See HORNS, *Section 9*, and WILD GAME, *Section 1*.)

He maketh my feet like hinds' [doe's] *feet: and setteth me upon my high places* (2 Samuel 22:34).

DOG—*Strife:* Contention; offense; unclean spirit. **Personal Pet** = *Something precious, or a friend* (as in "man's best friend"). **Dog Wagging Tail** = *Friendly;* acceptance. **Tucked Tail** = *Guilt;* shame; cowardly. **Biting Pet** = *Rewarding evil for good* (as in "biting the hand that feeds him"); betrayal; unthankful. **Barking Dog** = *Warning;* incessant nuisance; annoyance. **Dog Trailing Game** = *Persistent;* obsession. **Rabid Dog** = *Single-minded pursuit of evil;* contagious evil; persecution; great danger.

But if ye bite and devour one another, take heed that ye be not consumed one of another (Galatians 5:15).

He that passeth by, and meddleth with strife belonging not to him, is like one that taketh a dog by the ears (Proverbs 26:17).

And they have rewarded me evil for good, and hatred for my love (Psalm 109:5).

For men [who are dogs] *shall be lovers of their own selves, covetous, boasters, proud, blasphemers, disobedient to parents, unthankful, unholy, without natural affection, trucebreakers, false accusers, incontinent, fierce, despisers of those that are good, traitors, heady, highminded, lovers of pleasures more than lovers of God* (2 Timothy 3:2-4).

BULLDOG—*Unyielding:* Stubborn; tenacious; dangerous.

And it came to pass, when the judge was dead, that they returned, and corrupted themselves more than their fathers, in following other gods to serve them, and to bow down unto them; they ceased not from their own doings, nor from their stubborn way (Judges 2:19).

WATCHDOG—*Watchman:* Elder; minister (good or bad); alert; beware.

His watchmen are blind: they are all ignorant, they are all dumb dogs, they cannot bark; sleeping, lying down, loving to slumber. Yea, they are greedy dogs which can never have enough, and they are shepherds that cannot understand... (Isaiah 56:10-11).

That thy foot may be dipped in the blood of thine enemies, and the tongue of thy dogs in the same (Psalm 68:23).

DONKEY—*Obnoxious:* Self-willed; stubborn; unyielding; tenacious. **Braying** = *Bragging.* (See MULE.)

A whip for the horse, a bridle for the ass, and a rod for the fool's back (Proverbs 26:3).

And when the ass saw the angel of the Lord, she thrust herself unto the wall, and crushed Balaam's foot against the wall: and he smote her again (Numbers 22:25).

But [Balaam] *was rebuked for his iniquity: the dumb ass speaking with man's voice forbad the madness of the prophet* (2 Peter 2:16).

DOVE—See BIRD.

EAGLE—*Leader:* Prophet (true or false); to see from above (as in "an eagle's eye view"); minister; fierce predator; sorcerer; America.

Ye have seen what I did unto the Egyptians, and how I bare you on eagles' wings, and brought you unto Myself [Hosea 12:13 reads: "And by a prophet the Lord brought Israel out of Egypt, and by a prophet was he preserved."] (Exodus 19:4).

Calling a ravenous bird from the east, the man that executeth my counsel from a far country... (Isaiah 46:11).

ELEPHANT—*Invincible or thick-skinned:* Not easily offended; powerful; large. **Elephant Ears** = *Extra sensitive hearing.* **Baby Elephant** = *Potential for greatness* (the beginning of something large). **White Elephant** = *Unusable item;* unsalable; unwanted.

I can do all things through Christ which strengtheneth me [compare Romans 8:37, "Nay, in all these things we are more than conquerors through Him that loved us"] (Philippians 4:13).

FISH—*Spirit or Soul:* Person (good or bad); a person's character or motive (as in "something sure smells fishy about him"); Holy Spirit; unclean spirit. (See FISHING, *Section 9.*)

Again, the kingdom of heaven is like unto a net, that was cast into the sea, and gathered [fish, i.e., souls] *of every kind: which, when it was full, they drew to shore, and sat down, and gathered the good into vessels, but cast the bad away* (Matthew 13:47-48).

If a son shall ask bread of any of you that is a father, will he give him a stone? or if he ask a fish, will he for a fish give him a serpent? (Luke 11:11)

FLEA—*Insignificant:* Nuisance; irritant; elusive.

After whom is the king of Israel come out? after whom dost thou pursue? after a dead dog, after a flea (1 Samuel 24:14).

FLY—*Unclean:* Corruption; demon; curse; nuisance.

Dead flies cause the ointment of the apothecary to send forth a stinking savor: so doth a little folly him that is in reputation for wisdom and honor (Ecclesiastes 10:1).

And the Lord did so; and there came a grievous swarm of flies into the house of Pharaoh, and into his servants' houses, and into all the land of Egypt: the land was corrupted by reason of the swarm of flies (Exodus 8:24).

FOX—*Subtlety:* Deception; cunning; also, a con man; false prophet; wicked leader; hidden sin (as in "foxes have holes," i.e., they hide).

Take us the foxes, the little foxes [subtle deception of the enemy or secret sins], *that spoil the vines: for our vines have tender grapes* (Song of Solomon 2:15).

And He said unto them, Go ye, and tell that fox [Herod, the sly, wicked king], *Behold, I cast out devils...* (Luke 13:32).

O Israel, thy prophets are like the foxes in the deserts. ... They have seen vanity and lying divination, saying, The Lord saith: and the Lord hath not sent them: and they have made others to hope that they would confirm the word (Ezekiel 13:4,6).

FROG—*Spirit:* Demon; witchcraft; curse; evil words (as in "casting a spell"); puffed up.

He sent...frogs, which destroyed them (Psalm 78:45).

And I saw three unclean spirits like frogs come out of the mouth [released and expressed through words] *of the dragon, and out of the mouth of the beast, and out of the mouth of the false prophet* (Revelation 16:13).

GOAT—*Sinner:* Unbelief; stubborn; unyielding; strife; argumentative, negative person; scapegoat (blamed for other's wrongdoing).

And He shall set the sheep on His right hand, but the goats [sinners] *on the left* (Matthew 25:33).

But the goat, on which the lot fell to be the scapegoat, shall be presented alive before the Lord, to make an atonement with him, and to let him go for a scapegoat [to be blamed or cursed for the wrongs of others] *into the wilderness* (Leviticus 16:10).

HAWK—*Predator:* Sorcerer; evil spirit; a person who is for war. **Falcon** = *Hunter;* minister. (See EAGLE.)

Also of your own selves shall men [eagles or hawks, i.e., predators] *arise, speaking perverse things, to draw away disciples after them* (Acts 20:30).

He was a mighty hunter before [in the face of, i.e., against] *the Lord: wherefore it is said, Even as Nimrod the mighty hunter* [predator] *before* [against] *the Lord* [i.e., one who hunts the souls of men to build his own kingdom] (Genesis 10:9).

HOG—See SWINE.

HORNET (or Wasp)—*Affliction:* Stinging, biting words; slander; strife; curse (because of sin); persecution; trouble; offense; demon spirits. (See BEES.)

Moreover the Lord thy God will send the hornet among them, until they that are left, and hide themselves from thee, be destroyed (Deuteronomy 7:20).

HORSE—*Time/Work:* Flesh (as in "the works of the flesh"); the work of God's Spirit through man; spiritual warfare; one week (or another specific period of time); age; strength.

They were as fed horses in the morning: every one neighed after his neighbor's wife [their works were works of the flesh; compare Galatians 5:19, "Now the works of the flesh are manifest, which are these; adultery, fornication, uncleanness, lasciviousness."] (Jeremiah 5:8).

An horse is a vain thing for safety: neither shall he deliver any by his great strength (Psalm 33:17).

HORSE'S RIDER—*Nature of time or work:* Anxious; happy; confident.

Then she saddled an ass, and said to her servant [in anguish of spirit], *Drive, and go forward; slack not thy riding for me, except I bid thee* (2 Kings 4:24).

And I saw, and behold a white horse: and he that sat on him had a bow; and a crown was given unto him: and he went forth conquering, and to conquer (Revelation 6:2).

And I looked, and behold a pale horse: and his name that sat on him was Death, and Hell followed with him (Revelation 6:8a).

FRONT HALF OF HORSE—*First part of time or work:* Beginning; ready.

BACK HALF OF HORSE—*Last part of time or work:* End; also, an offensive or obnoxious person.

BLACK HORSE—*Famine:* Bad times; evil. (See BLACK, *Section 3.*)

And when he had opened the third seal, I heard the third beast say, Come and see. And I beheld, and lo a black horse; and he that sat on him had a pair of balances in his hand (Revelation 6:5).

Behold, the days come, saith the Lord God, that I will send a famine in the land, not a famine of bread, nor a thirst for water, but of hearing the words of the Lord (Amos 8:11).

RED HORSE—*Persecution:* Anger; danger; opposition. (See RED, *Section 3.*)

And there went out another horse that was red: and power was given to him that sat thereon to take peace from the earth, and that they should kill one another: and there was given unto him a great sword (Revelation 6:4).

They shall put you out of the synagogues: yea, the time cometh, that whosoever killeth you will think that he doeth God service (John 16:2).

KICKING/LIFTING HEEL—*Threatening:* Betrayal; rebellion; persecution.

I speak not of you all: I know whom I have chosen: but that the scripture may be fulfilled, He that eateth bread with Me hath lifted up his heel against Me (John 13:18).

QUARTER HORSE—*Strong:* Good times; fast; agility; success.

And I saw, and behold a white [or quarter] *horse: and he that sat on him had a bow; and a crown was given unto him: and he went forth conquering, and to conquer* (Revelation 6:2).

HOUND—See DOG.

KANGAROO—*To jump:* Predisposition; prejudiced (as in "a Kangaroo Court," where the verdict is decided before the person is even tried); to jump to a conclusion; Australia.

He that answereth a matter before he heareth it, it is folly and shame unto him (Proverbs 18:13).

Then shalt thou inquire, and make search, and ask diligently; and, behold, if it be truth, and the thing certain, that such abomination is wrought among you [See Deuteronomy 17:8-13.] (Deuteronomy 13:14).

LEOPARD—*Powerful:* Powerful leader (good or evil); predator; permanent, unchanging evil person; danger. (See LION.)

...A leopard shall watch over their cities: every one that goeth out thence shall be torn in pieces: because their transgressions are many, and their backslidings are increased (Jeremiah 5:6).

Can the Ethiopian change his skin, or the leopard his spots? then may ye also do good, that are accustomed to do evil (Jeremiah 13:23).

LICE—*Conviction:* Shame; guilt; accusation; affliction. (See FINGER, *Section 9.*)

...Aaron stretched out his hand with his rod, and smote the dust of the earth, and it became lice in man, and in beast; all the dust of the land became lice throughout all the land of Egypt. ... Then the magicians said unto Pharaoh, This is the finger [accusation] *of God: and Pharaoh's heart was hardened* [refused the conviction of God's Spirit], *and he hearkened not unto them...* (Exodus 8:17,19).

This they said, tempting Him, that they might have to accuse Him. But Jesus stooped down, and with His finger wrote on the [dust of the] *ground, as though He heard them not. ... And they which heard it, being convicted* [accused] *by their own conscience, went out* [ashamed, as one afflicted and infected by lice] *one by one, beginning at the eldest, even unto the last: and Jesus was left alone, and the woman standing in the midst* (John 8:6,9).

LION—*Dominion:* Christ; king; regal; bold; power; satan; religious tradition; destroying spirit. (See LEOPARD.)

And one of the elders saith unto me, Weep not: behold, the Lion of the tribe of Judah [Christ], *the Root of David, hath prevailed to open the book, and to loose the seven seals thereof* (Revelation 5:5).

A lion which is strongest among beasts, and turneth not away for any (Proverbs 30:30).

The wicked flee when no man pursueth: but the righteous are bold as a lion (Proverbs 28:1).

Be sober, be vigilant; because your adversary the devil, as a roaring lion, walketh about, seeking whom he may devour (1 Peter 5:8).

Beware lest any man spoil you [devour you or your blessings] *through philosophy and vain deceit, after the* [religious] *tradition of men, after the rudiments of the world, and not after Christ* (Colossians 2:8).

MAGGOT—*Corruption:* Filthiness of the flesh; evil.

But I am a worm [Heb.: "maggot"], *and no man; a reproach of men, and despised of the people* (Psalm 22:6).

MICE—*Devourer:* Curse; plague; timid (as in "Are you a man or a mouse?").

Then said they, What shall be the trespass offering which we shall return to him? They answered, Five golden emerods, and five golden mice...for one plague was on you all, and on your lords (1 Samuel 6:4).

And I will rebuke the devourer for your sakes, and he shall not destroy the fruits of your ground (Malachi 3:11a).

For God hath not given us the spirit of fear [Gk.: "timidity"]; *but of power, and of love, and of a sound mind* (2 Timothy 1:7).

MONKEY—*Foolishness or Clinging:* Mischief; dishonesty (as in "monkey business"); addiction (i.e., a heroin addict is said to "have a monkey on his back").

Though thou shouldest bray a fool in a mortar among wheat with a pestle, yet will not his foolishness depart from him (Proverbs 27:22).

They have stricken me, shalt thou say, and I was not sick; they have beaten me, and I felt it not: when shall I awake? I will seek it [wine or any addictive substance] *yet again* (Proverbs 23:35).

MOTH—*Deterioration:* (*Note:* A moth is an insect of darkness.) Loss through deceit; secret or undetected trouble; corruption; chastisement.

Therefore will I be unto Ephraim as a moth, and to the house of Judah as rottenness (Hosea 5:12).

Lay not up for yourselves treasures upon earth, where moth and rust doth corrupt (Matthew 6:19a).

MULE—*Stubborn:* Self-willed; tenacious; strong; also, unbelief (See DONKEY.)

Be ye not as the horse, or as the mule, which have no understanding: whose mouth must be held in with bit and bridle... (Psalm 32:9).

But they refused to hearken, and pulled away the shoulder, and stopped their ears, that they should not hear (Zechariah 7:11).

OWL—*Circumspect (looking around):* Wisdom (as in "a wise old owl"); also, demon (because it is a bird of the night); curse.

And in all things that I have said unto you be circumspect (Exodus 23:13a).

And thorns [curses] *shall come up in her palaces...and it shall be...a court for owls* (Isaiah 34:13).

PARROT—*Mimic:* Copy; mock; repeat.

And he [Elisha] *went up from thence unto Bethel: and as he was going up by the way, there came forth little children out of the city, and mocked him, and said unto him, Go up, thou bald head; go up, thou bald head* (2 Kings 2:23).

PIG—See SWINE.

RABBIT—*Increase:* Fast growth; multiplication (good or evil increase). (See WILD GAME, *Section 1.*)

An inheritance may be gotten hastily at the beginning: but the end thereof shall not be blessed (Proverbs 20:21).

RACCOON—*Mischief:* Night raider; rascal; thief; bandit; deceitful; obsession with or excessive cleanliness.

For they sleep not, except they have done mischief (Proverbs 4:16a).

It is as sport to a fool to do mischief (Proverbs 10:23a).

RAT—*Unclean:* Wicked person; jerk; devourer; plague (curse because of sin); betrayer (as in "ratting on someone"). (See MICE.)

Whoso [is a rat and] *rewardeth evil for good, evil shall not depart from his house* (Proverbs 17:13).

The wicked plotteth against the just, and gnasheth upon him with his teeth (Psalm 37:12).

And if ye walk contrary unto Me, and will not hearken unto Me; I will bring seven times more plagues [such as bubonic plague, carried by rats] *upon you according to your sins* (Leviticus 26:21).

ROACHES—*Infestation:* Unclean spirits; uncleanness; hidden sin.

Having therefore these promises, dearly beloved, let us cleanse ourselves from all filthiness of the flesh and spirit (2 Corinthians 7:1a).

SCORPION—*Sin Nature:* Lust of the flesh; temptation; deception; accusation; destruction; danger.

Behold, I give unto you power to tread on serpents and scorpions [the sin nature of the flesh], *and over all the power of the enemy: and nothing shall by any means hurt you* (Luke 10:19).

The [scorpion's] *sting of death is sin; and the strength of sin is the law* (1 Corinthians 15:56).

But I see another law in my members, warring against the law of my mind, and bringing me into captivity to the law [or nature] *of sin* [the scorpion] *which is in my members* (Romans 7:23).

SHEEP—*Innocent:* Saint(s); unsaved person(s).

But go rather to the lost sheep of the house of Israel (Matthew 10:6).

And David spake unto the Lord when he saw the angel that smote the people, and said, Lo, I have sinned, and I have done wickedly: but these sheep [innocent people], *what have they done?* (2 Samuel 24:17a)

And He shall set the sheep [innocent, saved people] *on His right hand, but the goats* [guilty, unsaved people] *on the left* (Matthew 25:33).

SLOTH—*Lazy:* Lethargic; lifeless; slow.

But if any provide not for his own, and specially for those of his own house, he hath denied the faith, and is worse than an infidel (1 Timothy 5:8).

He also that is slothful in his work is brother to him that is a great waster (Proverbs 18:9).

By much slothfulness the building decayeth; and through idleness of the hands the house droppeth through (Ecclesiastes 10:18).

SNAKE—*Curse:* Demon; deception; threat; danger; hatred; slander; critical spirit; witchcraft. **Fangs** = *Evil intent;* danger. **Rattles** = *Words;* threats; warning; alarm. (See BEAR.)

And the Lord God said unto the serpent, Because thou hast done this, thou art cursed above all cattle, and above every beast of the field (Genesis 3:14a).

As if a man did flee from a lion, and a bear met him; or went into the house, and leaned his hand on the wall, and a serpent bit him (Amos 5:19).

They have sharpened their tongues like a serpent [slander]; *adders' poison is under their lips...* (Psalm 140:3).

At the last it [alcohol] *biteth like a serpent, and stingeth like an adder* (Proverbs 23:32).

And that [the person] *which is crushed breaketh out into a viper* [becomes bitter, critical, etc.] (Isaiah 59:5b).

SPIDER (WEB)—*Evil:* Sin; deception; false doctrine; temptation. **Web** = *Snare;* lies (as in "what tangled webs we weave when first we practice to deceive"). (See SCORPION.)

There be four things which are little upon the earth, but they are exceeding wise. ... The spider taketh hold with her hands [works (see Rom. 6:16)], *and is in kings' palaces* (Proverbs 30:24,28).

And I find more bitter than death the woman, whose heart is snares and nets, and her hands as bands [or webs]*: whoso pleaseth God shall escape from her; but the sinner shall be taken by her* (Ecclesiastes 7:26).

BLACK WIDOW—*Danger:* Great danger; deadly; evil; slander.

But the tongue can no man tame; it is an unruly evil, full of deadly poison (James 3:8).

STORK—*Expectant:* New birth; new baby; new experience; that which is forthcoming.

Yea, the stork in the heaven knoweth her appointed times...but My people know not the judgment of the Lord (Jeremiah 8:7).

SWINE—*Unclean:* Selfish; backslider; unbeliever; glutton; fornicator; hypocrite; idolater. **Boar** = *Persecutor;* hostile to virtue; vicious; vengeful; danger.

But it is happened unto them according to the true proverb, The dog is turned to his own vomit again; and the sow that was washed to her wallowing in the mire (2 Peter 2:22).

Give not that which is holy unto the dogs, neither cast ye your pearls before swine, lest they trample them under their feet, and turn again and rend you (Matthew 7:6).

The boar out of the wood [i.e., from among the people] *doth waste it, and the wild beast of the field doth devour it* (Psalm 80:13).

For men shall be lovers of their own selves, covetous, boasters, proud, blasphemers, disobedient to parents, unthankful, unholy, without natural affection, trucebreakers, false accusers, incontinent, fierce, despisers of those that are good [Gk.: "hostile to virtue"] (2 Timothy 3:2-3).

TERMITES—*Corruption:* Hidden destruction; secret sin; deception; demon spirits. (See MOTH.)

If the foundations be destroyed, what can the righteous do? (Psalm 11:3)

Ye have sown much, and bring in little; ye eat, but ye have not enough; ye drink, but ye are not filled with drink; ye clothe you, but there is none warm; and he that earneth wages earneth wages to put it into a bag with holes [as termites eat the strength of the walls of a house, causing damage and loss] (Haggai 1:6).

TERRAPIN—*Slow:* Withdrawn; cautious; protected; safe.

Wherefore, my beloved brethren, let every man be swift to hear, slow to speak, slow to wrath (James 1:19).

TICK—*Hidden:* Hidden unclean spirit; oblivious to one's true self (as in practicing self-justification and self-righteousness); parasite; pest.

Or if a soul touch any unclean thing...or the carcass of unclean creeping things, and if it be hidden from him; he also shall be unclean, and guilty (Leviticus 5:2).

The heart is deceitful above all things, and desperately wicked: who can know it? (Jeremiah 17:9)

TIGER—*Danger:* Powerful minister (danger for the devil!); evil, dangerous person (good or evil). (See LEOPARD.)

He that committeth sin is of the devil; for the devil sinneth from the beginning. For this purpose the Son of God was manifested, that He might destroy the works of the devil (1 John 3:8).

TURKEY—*Foolish:* Dumb; clumsy (in word or deed); thanksgiving.

For man also knoweth not his time...as the birds that are caught in the snare; so are the sons of men snared in an evil time, when it falleth suddenly upon them (Ecclesiastes 9:12).

VULTURE—*Scavenger:* Unclean; impure; an evil person; also, all seeing; waiting (in an evil sense, as a person waiting for parents to die so he/she may get their possessions).

But these are they [which are unclean] *of which ye shall not eat: the eagle...and the vulture after his kind* (Deuteronomy 14:12-13).

The eye that mocketh at his father, and despiseth to obey his mother, the ravens of the valley shall pick it out, and the young eagles [or vultures] *shall eat it* (Proverbs 30:17).

WASP—See HORNET.

WEASEL—*Wicked:* Renege on a promise (as in "weasel out of a deal"); informant or tattletale (as in "that weasel squealed on me"); a Judas (betrayer); traitor; informant.

And Judas Iscariot, one of the twelve, went unto the chief priests, to betray Him unto them (Mark 14:10).

WILD GAME—*Work:* **Hunting or Eating Deer, Birds, etc.** = *Seeking or doing God's Word and work;* sorcery. (See FOOD/MILK, TEETH and subheadings, *Section 9.*)

The slothful man roasteth not that which he took in hunting [he does not meditate on and act upon the revelation knowledge he receives from his studies of the Word of God]*: but the substance of a diligent man is precious* (Proverbs 12:27).

WOLF—*Predator:* Devourer; false prophet; evil minister or governor; person seeking his own gain; womanizer; God's minister of justice. **Fangs** = *Evil motive;* danger.

Beware of false prophets, which come to you in sheep's clothing, but inwardly they are ravening wolves (Matthew 7:15).

For I know this, that after my departing shall grievous wolves enter in among you, not sparing the flock. Also of your own selves shall men arise, speaking perverse things, to draw away disciples after them (Acts 20:29-30).

WORM—See MAGGOT.

2

Buildings/Rooms/Places

AIRPORT—*Waiting:* Preparing; being made ready (for ministry, travel, change, etc.); also, the Church.

Which sometime were disobedient, when once the longsuffering of God waited in the days of Noah, while the ark was a preparing, wherein few, that is, eight souls were saved by water (1 Peter 3:20).

But if they had stood in My counsel [waited for God's training and preparation in them to be completed], *and had caused My people to hear My words, then they should have turned them from their evil way, and from the evil of their doings* (Jeremiah 23:22).

ATTIC—*Mind:* Thought; attitude (good or bad); learning; spiritual realm. **Dusty Relics From the Past** = *Memories.*

Peter went up upon the housetop to pray...he fell into a trance, and saw heaven opened, and a certain vessel descending unto him, as it had been a great sheet knit at the four corners, and let down to the earth (Acts 10:9b-11).

Brethren, I count not myself to have apprehended: but this one thing I do, forgetting those things which are behind, and reaching forth unto those things which are before (Philippians 3:13).

BANK—*Secure:* Dependable; safe; saved; certain (as in "you can bank on it"); reward reserved in heaven; the Church.

Wherefore then gavest not thou my money [talents, spiritual gifts, etc.] *into the bank* [submitted one's gifts and abilities to those whom God has placed in spiritual authority], *that at my coming I might have required mine own with usury?* (Luke 19:23)

But lay up for yourselves treasures in heaven...where thieves do not break through nor steal (Matthew 6:20).

BARBERSHOP—*Church:* Place of removal of old covenants of sin, occult, or religion. **Haircut** = *Putting away tradition or bad habits;* repenting of bad attitudes. (See HAIR, BEARD, *Section 9,* and BEAUTY SHOP, *Section 2.*)

That he told her all his heart, and said unto her, There hath not come a razor upon mine head; for I have been a Nazarite unto God from my mother's womb: if I be shaven [break the covenant], *then my strength will go from me, and I shall become weak, and be like any other man* (Judges 16:17).

And be not conformed to this world: but be ye transformed by the renewing of your mind (Romans 12:2a).

BARN—*Storehouse:* Church; relating to the work of the ministry; provision; large work. (See HAY, *Section 9.*)

Let both grow together until the harvest: and in the time of harvest I will say to the reapers, Gather ye together first the tares [hypocrites], *and bind them in bundles to burn them:*

but gather the wheat [righteous] *into my barn* (Matthew 13:30).

Where no oxen are, the crib [or barn] *is clean: but much increase is by the strength of the ox* [ministry] (Proverbs 14:4).

And he said, This will I do: I will pull down my barns, and build greater [megachurches]; *and there will I bestow all my fruits and my goods* (Luke 12:18).

BASEMENT—*Soul:* Carnal nature; lust; discouragement or depression; refuge; retreat; hidden; forgotten; secret sin; put away or stored (as in "put away in the basement"). (See FOUNDATION.)

Then took they Jeremiah, and cast him into the dungeon...and they let down Jeremiah with cords. And in the dungeon there was no water, but mire: so Jeremiah sunk in the mire (Jeremiah 38:6).

BATHROOM—*Desire or Cleansing:* Prayer of repentance; confession of offenses or sins to another person; passion; strong lust.

Wash you, make you clean; put away the evil of your doings from before Mine eyes; cease to do evil (Isaiah 1:16).

The beginning of strife [or sexual lust] *is as when one letteth out water: therefore leave off contention* [and lust], *before it be meddled with* (Proverbs 17:14).

...David arose from off his bed, and walked upon the roof of the king's house: and from the roof he saw a woman washing herself; and the woman was very beautiful to look upon. ... And David sent messengers, and took her; and she came in unto him, and he lay with her; for she was purified from her uncleanness... (2 Samuel 11:2,4).

BEAUTY SHOP—*Church:* Preparation; vanity; holiness. (See BARBERSHOP.)

The inhabitants of Samaria [mixed, incorrect worship] *shall fear because of the calves of Bethaven* [(a play on words) *Bethaven* = house of vanity; i.e., as opposed to Bethel, the house of God]: *for the people thereof shall mourn over it, and the priests thereof that rejoiced on it, for the glory thereof, because it is departed from it* (Hosea 10:5).

Favor is deceitful, and beauty is vain: but a woman that feareth the Lord, she shall be praised (Proverbs 31:30).

But if a woman have long hair, it is a glory to her: for her hair is given her for a covering (1 Corinthians 11:15).

Give unto the Lord the glory due unto His name; worship the Lord in the beauty of holiness (Psalm 29:2).

BEDROOM—*Rest:* Salvation; meditation; intimacy; privacy; peace; covenant (as in marriage), or an evil covenant (as in natural or spiritual adultery); self-made (harmful) conditions (as in "you made your bed, now sleep in it").

Stand in awe, and sin not: commune with your own heart upon your bed, and be still… (Psalm 4:4).

If I ascend up into heaven, Thou art there: if I make my bed in hell, behold, Thou art there [See Isaiah 28:18-20.] (Psalm 139:8).

Marriage is honorable in all, and the bed [is to be kept] *undefiled: but whoremongers and adulterers God will judge* (Hebrews 13:4).

Ye adulterers and adulteresses, know ye not that the friendship of the world is enmity with God? (James 4:4a)

BUILDING FRAME (a house under construction)— See FOUNDATION.

BUS STATION—See AIRPORT.

CAFETERIA—*Service:* Church; people or work; teaching; ministry of helps.

For I was an hungered, and ye gave Me meat: I was thirsty, and ye gave Me drink: I was a stranger, and ye took Me in (Matthew 25:35).

CHURCH BUILDING—*Church:* Congregation; may represent one's own Church. (See CHURCH SERVICE, *Section 9.*)

And I say also unto thee, That thou art Peter, and upon this rock I will build My church; and the gates of hell shall not prevail against it (Matthew 16:18).

CITY—*Characteristic:* That for which the city is known (for example: **Las Vegas** = *Gambling, prostitution, etc.*); the Church; a person's character.

Even as Sodom and Gomorrha...giving themselves over to fornication, and going after strange flesh, are set forth for an example, suffering the vengeance of eternal fire (Compare Ezekiel 16:49-50: "Behold, this was the iniquity of thy sister Sodom, pride, fullness of bread, and abundance of idleness was in her and in her daughters, neither did she strengthen the hand of the poor and needy. And they were haughty, and committed abomination [homosexuality] before Me: therefore I took them away as I saw good.") (Jude 1:7).

Save that the Holy Ghost witnesseth in every city [Church], *saying that bonds and afflictions abide me* (Acts 20:23).

He that hath no rule over his own spirit is like a city that is broken down, and without walls (Proverbs 25:28).

CONCRETE SLAB—See FOUNDATION.

COUNTRY—*Isolated:* Quiet; peaceful; restful; removed from the city. (A country, see NATION.)

And He said unto them, Come ye yourselves apart into a desert [or country] *place, and rest a while: for there were many coming and going, and they had no leisure so much as to eat* (Mark 6:31).

COURTHOUSE—*Judgment:* Trial; persecution; justice; legal matter. (See JUDGE, LAWYER, *Section 7,* and MISCARRIAGE, *Section 9.*)

Judges and officers shalt thou make thee in all thy gates [places of judgment], *which the Lord thy God giveth thee, throughout thy tribes: and they shall judge the people with just judgment* [See Deuteronomy 17:6-13.] (Deuteronomy 16:18).

I have declared, and have saved, and I have shown, when there was no strange god among you: therefore ye are My witnesses, saith the Lord, that I am God (Isaiah 43:12).

Shall the throne of iniquity [evil court] *have fellowship with Thee, which frameth mischief by a law?* (Psalm 94:20)

Dare any of you, having a matter against another, go to law before the unjust, and not before the saints? [See Matthew 18:15-19.] (1 Corinthians 6:1)

DEN—See LIVING ROOM.

FACTORY—*Production:* Getting things done; the Kingdom of God; the Church; the "world"; the motions of sin. **Idle Factory** = *Not busy;* not reaching full potential; natural workplace (when applicable). (See MACHINES, *Section 9.*)

> *And He said unto them, How is it that ye sought Me? wist ye not that I must be about My Father's business?* (Luke 2:49)

> · *Not slothful in business; fervent in spirit; serving the Lord* (Romans 12:11).

FARM—See FARMER, *Section 7.*

FOUNDATION—*Foundation (as in "a concrete slab for a building under construction"):* Established; stable; unstable (when shaky); not ready to proceed with construction (when incomplete); the gospel; sound doctrine; church government; building program.

> *If the foundations be destroyed, what can the righteous do?* (Psalm 11:3)

> *Lest haply, after he hath laid the foundation, and is not able to finish it, all that behold it begin to mock him* (Luke 14:29).

> *According to the grace of God which is given unto me, as a wise masterbuilder, I have laid the foundation, and another buildeth thereon.... For other foundation can no man lay than that is laid, which is Jesus Christ* [See Hebrews 6:1-2.] (1 Corinthians 3:10-11).

> *And are built upon the foundation of the apostles and prophets, Jesus Christ Himself being the chief corner stone* (Ephesians 2:20).

GROUND FLOOR—See LIVING ROOM.

HOSPITAL—*Care:* Church; place of healing; mercy; persons who are wounded or sick.

> *And Jesus answering said, A certain man went down from Jerusalem to Jericho, and fell among thieves, which... wounded him, and departed, leaving him half dead. ... But a certain Samaritan...had compassion on him, and went to him, and bound up his wounds, pouring in oil and wine...and brought him to an inn* [or hospital], *and took care of him* (Luke 10:30,33-34).

> *For I am poor and needy, and my heart is wounded within me* [Compare Psalm 147:3: "He healeth the broken in heart, and bindeth up their wounds."] (Psalm 109:22).

> *But He* [Jesus] *was wounded for our transgressions, He was bruised for our iniquities: the chastisement of our peace was upon Him; and with His stripes we are healed* (Isaiah 53:5).

HOTEL—*Public place for rest or business:* Church (place for rest in Christ); public gathering; travel; business travel.

> *And from thence, when the brethren heard of us, they came to meet us as far as Appii forum, and The three taverns: whom when Paul saw, he thanked God, and took courage* (Acts 28:15).

HOUSE—*Person or family:* Individual; Church. When naturally interpreted, it means a dwelling place. **Home** = *Heart* (as in "home is where the heart is"); identity; roots.

> *When the unclean spirit is gone out of a man, he walketh through dry places, seeking rest; and finding none, he saith,*

I will return unto my house [the person] *whence I came out* (Luke 11:24).

And they said, Believe on the Lord Jesus Christ, and thou shalt be saved, and thy house [family] (Acts 16:31).

For I have not dwelt in an house [made with hands] *since the day that I brought up Israel unto this day; but have gone from tent to tent, and from one tabernacle to another* [i.e., from one Church to another and from one person to another] (1 Chronicles 17:5).

NEW HOUSE—*New life (as in salvation):* Change; revival; new move (natural or spiritual). (See MOVING VAN, *Section 8.*)

Therefore if any man be in Christ, he is a new creature [or creation, i.e., new house]: *old things are passed away; behold, all things are become new* (2 Corinthians 5:17).

For we know that if our earthly house of this tabernacle [our body] *were dissolved* [by death], *we have a building of God, an house not made with hands, eternal in the heavens* (2 Corinthians 5:1).

OLD HOUSE—*Past:* Inheritance, e.g., one's Grandfather's or Grandmother's religion, ways, or temperament; established tradition. **An old house in good condition** = *God's ways;* righteousness; diligence. **In bad condition** = *Our sins or the sins of our forefathers.* Needing revival (when in need of repair or remodeling); untended (when unpainted or the property is grown over with weeds); neglect; unusable (when beyond repair); ruin. (See GRANDMOTHER, *Section 7.*)

Now the Lord had said unto Abram, Get thee out of thy country, and from thy kindred, and from thy father's house [natural and spiritual inheritance], *unto a land that I will show thee* (Genesis 12:1).

Thus saith the Lord, Stand ye in the ways, and see, and ask for the old paths [or the old house of God], *where is the good way, and walk therein, and ye shall find rest for your souls...* (Jeremiah 6:16).

HOUSE TRAILER—*Temporary:* Place; situation; relationship.

Whereas ye know not what shall be on the morrow. For what is your life? It is even a vapor, that appeareth for a little time, and then vanisheth away (James 4:14).

HOUSE UNDER CONSTRUCTION—See FOUNDATION.

JAIL—See PRISON.

KITCHEN—*Heart:* Intent; motive; plans; passion; ambition; affliction (as in "if you can't take the heat, stay out of the kitchen"). (See OVEN and REFRIGERATOR, *Section 9.*)

For they have made ready their heart like an oven, whiles they lie in wait: their baker sleepeth all the night; in the morning it burneth as a flaming fire (Hosea 7:6).

For the word of God is quick, and powerful, and sharper than any twoedged sword, piercing even to the dividing asunder of soul and spirit, and of the joints and marrow, and is a discerner of the thoughts and intents of the heart [where things are cooked up, or planned] (Hebrews 4:12).

LIBRARY—*Knowledge:* Education; learning; research; distraction (when noisy). (See BOOK and NOISE, *Section 9.*)

Study to show thyself approved unto God, a workman that needeth not to be ashamed, rightly dividing the word of truth (2 Timothy 2:15).

LIVING ROOM—*Revealed:* Everyday or current affairs; that which is manifest; truth exposed; without hypocrisy. (See PORCH.)

And when they could not come nigh unto Him for the press, they uncovered the roof where He was [living room]: *and when they had broken it up, they let down the bed wherein the sick of the palsy lay. When Jesus saw their faith, He said unto the sick of the palsy, Son, thy sins be forgiven thee* (Mark 2:4-5).

MOTEL—See HOTEL.

NATION (or Nationality)—*Characteristic:* That for which the people are known. Some examples are: **France** = *Romance.* **Germany** = *Industrious;* hardworking. **Israel (a Jew)** = *Shrewd business dealings* (as in "he jewed the price down"); persecuted. May represent the actual nation. (See CITY.)

Israel shall be a proverb and a byword among all people (1 Kings 9:7b).

PARK—*Rest:* Peace; God's blessing; God's provision (as in "the garden of Eden"); leisure; vagrancy.

And the Lord shall guide thee continually, and satisfy thy soul in drought, and make fat thy bones: and thou shalt be like a watered garden, and like a spring of water, whose waters fail not (Isaiah 58:11).

PORCH (FRONT)—*Public:* Open to everyone; exposed; revealed.

But he denied, saying, I know not, neither understand I what thou sayest. And he went out into the porch; and the cock crew [knew!] (Mark 14:68).

And by the hands of the apostles were many signs and wonders wrought among the people; (and they were all with one accord in Solomon's porch [public witness]*)* (Acts 5:12).

Let the priests, the ministers of the Lord, weep between the porch and the altar [public prayer and confession], *and let them say, Spare Thy people, O Lord...wherefore should they say among the people, Where is their God?* (Joel 2:17)

PRISON—*Bondage:* Rebellion; strong emotion (such as depression, fear, rebellion, hatred, etc.); addiction (alcoholic, dope, etc.). **Prisoners** = *Lost souls;* stubborn sinners; persecuted saints.

The Spirit of the Lord is upon Me, because He hath anointed Me to preach the gospel to the poor; He hath sent Me to heal the brokenhearted, to preach deliverance to the captives, and recovering of sight to the blind, to set at liberty them that are bruised (Luke 4:18).

And deliver them who through fear of death were all their lifetime subject to bondage (Hebrews 2:15).

Having eyes full of adultery, and that cannot cease from sin... (2 Peter 2:14).

In meekness instructing those that oppose themselves; if God peradventure will give them repentance to the acknowledging of the truth; and that they may recover themselves out of the snare of the devil, who are taken captive by him [the devil] *at His* [God's] *will* (2 Timothy 2:25-26).

Then took they Jeremiah, and cast him into the dungeon...that was in the court of the prison...so Jeremiah sunk in the mire (Jeremiah 38:6).

Turn you to the strong hold, ye prisoners of hope (Zechariah 9:12a).

ROOF—*Covering:* Protection; mind; thought.

What I tell you in darkness, that speak ye in light: and what ye hear in the ear, that preach ye upon the housetops (Matthew 10:27).

Woe to the rebellious children, saith the Lord, that take counsel, but not of Me; and that cover with a covering, but not of My spirit... (Isaiah 30:1).

And it came to pass in an eveningtide, that David arose from off his bed, and walked upon the roof of the king's house: and from the roof he saw a woman washing herself; and the woman was very beautiful to look upon (2 Samuel 11:2).

SCHOOL—*Teaching or learning:* Church; people or work; teaching ministry; training.

But when divers were hardened, and believed not, but spake evil of that way before the multitude, he departed from them, and separated the disciples [Church], *disputing daily in the school of one Tyrannus* (Acts 19:9).

Then they went out to see what was done; and came to Jesus, and found the man, out of whom the devils were departed, sitting at the feet of Jesus [being counseled or taught], *clothed, and in his right mind...* (Luke 8:35).

TRAIN STATION—See AIRPORT.

UPSTAIRS (or UPPER ROOM)—*Spiritual:* Thought (godly or carnal); prayer; spiritual service. (See ATTIC.)

And when they were come in, they went up into an upper room, where abode both Peter, and James, and John... .

These all continued with one accord in prayer and supplication... (Acts 1:13-14).

...Paul preached unto them...and continued his speech until midnight. And there were many lights in the upper chamber, where they were gathered together (Acts 20:7-8).

YARD--See BACK and FRONT, *Section 4.*

ZOO—*Strange:* Commotion; confusion; chaos; disarray (as in "this place is a regular zoo!"); very busy place; noisy strife (like a zoo at feeding time); **Family visit** = *Quality time with the family.*

And they were all amazed, and they glorified God, and were filled with fear, saying, We have seen strange things to day (Luke 5:26).

For where envying and strife is, there is confusion and every evil work (James 3:16).

3

Colors

BLACK—*Lack*: Sin; ignorance; grief; mourning; gloomy; evil; ominous; famine; burned.

For at the window of my house I looked...and beheld... among the youths, a young man void of understanding... and he went the way to [a harlot's] house, in the twilight, in the evening, in the black and dark night (Proverbs 7:6-9).

For the hurt of the daughter of My people am I hurt; I am black; astonishment hath taken hold on Me. Is there no balm in Gilead; is there no physician there? why then is not the health of the daughter of My people recovered? (Jeremiah 8:21-22)

Our skin was black like an oven because of the terrible famine [lack of substance] (Lamentations 5:10).

I am black, but comely, O ye daughters of Jerusalem, as the tents of Kedar, as the curtains of Solomon (Song of Solomon 1:5).

His head is as the most fine gold, his locks are bushy, and black as a raven (Song of Solomon 5:11).

BLUE—*Spiritual*: Spiritual gift; divine revelation; heavenly visitation; depressed (as in "singing the blues"); a male infant. **Medium or Dark Blue** = *God's Spirit or Word;* blessing; healing; good will. **Very Light Blue** = *Spirit of man;* evil spirit; corrupt.

> *And upon the table of showbread they shall spread a cloth of blue, and put thereon the dishes, and the spoons…. And they shall take a cloth of blue, and cover the candlestick of the light, and his lamps…and all the oil vessels thereof, wherewith they minister unto it* (Numbers 4:7,9).

> *Which were clothed with blue, captains and rulers, all of them desirable young men…* (Ezekiel 23:6).

> *The blueness of a wound cleanseth away evil* (Proverbs 20:30a).

> *And suddenly there was with the angel a multitude of the heavenly host praising God, and saying, Glory to God in the highest, and on earth peace, good will toward men* (Luke 2:13-14).

BROWN (or Tan)—*Dead (as dead grass is brown):* Repented; born again; without spirit.

> *For all flesh is as* [green] *grass, and all the glory of man as the flower of grass. The grass withereth* [turns brown in death, i.e., repentance]*, and the flower thereof falleth away* (1 Peter 1:24).

GRAY—*Not Defined:* Unclear (as in "the gray area between right and wrong"); vague, not specific; hazy; deceived; deception; hidden; crafty; false doctrine. **Gray Hair** = *Wisdom, age, or weakness.*

> *The hoary* [white or gray] *head is a crown of glory, if it be found in the way of righteousness* (Proverbs 16:31).

Strangers have devoured his strength, and he knoweth it not [deception]*: yea, gray hairs are here and there upon him, yet he knoweth not* (Hosea 7:9).

GREEN—*Life:* Mortal; flesh; carnal; envy; inexperienced; immature; renewal. **Evergreen** = *Eternal life;* immortal. (See GRASS and TREE, *Section 9.*)

Every moving thing that liveth shall be meat for you; even as the green herb have I given you all things (Genesis 9:3).

For all flesh is as [green] *grass, and all the glory of man as the flower of grass. The grass withereth, and the flower thereof falleth away* (1 Peter 1:24).

I have seen the wicked in great power, and spreading himself like a green bay tree (Psalm 37:35).

For if they do these things in a green tree [mortal days of Christ flesh], *what shall be done in the dry* [after His death, without His physical presence]*?* (Luke 23:31)

ORANGE—*Danger:* Great jeopardy; harm. (A common color combination is orange and black together, which usually signifies great evil or danger). **Bright or Fire Orange** = *Power;* force; energy; energetic; danger.

But I say unto you, That whosoever is angry with his brother without a cause shall be in danger of the judgment…but whosoever shall say, Thou fool, shall be in danger of hell fire [fire is orange] (Matthew 5:22).

Can a man take fire in his bosom, and his clothes not be burned? (Proverbs 6:27)

PINK—*Flesh:* Sensual; sensuous (as in "hot pink bikini"); immoral; moral (as in "a heart of flesh"); chaste; a female infant.

A new heart also will I give you, and a new spirit will I put within you: and I will take away the stony [hard] heart out of your flesh, and I will give you an [pink (chaste, virtuous)] heart of flesh [Compare Second Corinthians 11:2: "...I have espoused you to one husband, that I may present you as a chaste virgin to Christ."] (Ezekiel 36:26).

PURPLE—*Royal:* Rule (good or evil); majestic; noble.

And purple raiment that was on the kings of Midian... (Judges 8:26b).

And they clothed Him with purple, and platted a crown of thorns, and put it about His head (Mark 15:17).

RED—*Passion:* Emotion; anger; hatred; lust; sin; enthusiasm; zeal.

And there went out another horse that was red: and power was given to him that sat thereon to take peace from the earth, and that they should kill one another: and there was given unto him a great sword [See James 4:1.] (Revelation 6:4).

Come now, and let us reason together, saith the Lord: though your sins be as scarlet, they shall be as white as snow; though they be red like crimson, they shall be as wool (Isaiah 1:18).

TAN—See BROWN.

WHITE—*Pure:* Without mixture; unblemished; spotless; righteousness; blameless; truth; innocence.

And to her was granted that she should be arrayed in fine linen, clean and white: for the fine linen is the righteousness of saints (Revelation 19:8).

The leprosy therefore of Naaman shall cleave unto thee...and he went out from his presence a leper as white as snow [cursed, completely covered, without mixture, i.e., without mercy] (2 Kings 5:27).

YELLOW—*Gift:* A gift (with feeling); gift from or of God; marriage; family; honor; deceitful gift; timidity; fear; cowardliness. Welcome home (as in "a yellow ribbon"). (See ROSE, *Section 9.*)

Though ye have lain among the pots, yet shall ye be as the wings of a dove [spiritual] *covered with silver* [knowledge], *and her feathers with yellow gold* [spirit of wisdom and the glory of God] (Psalm 68:13).

House and riches are the inheritance of fathers: and a prudent wife is [a gift] *from the Lord* (Proverbs 19:14).

For God hath not given us the spirit of fear; but of power, and of love, and of a sound mind (2 Timothy 1:7).

4

Directions

BACK (as in **Backyard** or **Back Door**)—*Past:* Previous event or experience (good or evil); that which is behind (in time: for example, your past sins or the sins of your forefathers); unaware; unsuspecting; hidden; memory. (See DOOR, *Section 9.*)

And Abraham...looked, and behold behind him a ram caught in a thicket by his horns: and Abraham...offered him up for a burnt offering in the stead of his son [Compare John 8:58: "Jesus said unto them, Verily, verily, I say unto you, Before {behind, i.e., before in time} Abraham was, I am."] (Genesis 22:13).

And he commanded them, saying, Behold, ye shall lie in wait against the city, even [hidden] *behind the city...* (Joshua 8:4).

Brethren, I count not myself to have apprehended: but this one thing I do, forgetting those things which are behind [of the past], *and reaching forth unto those things which are before* (Philippians 3:13).

EAST (Heb: "In front of you when facing the rising sun")—*Beginning:* Law of Moses (therefore blessed or cursed); birth; first; anticipate; false religion (as in "Eastern religions").

And it came to pass, as they journeyed from the east [beginning, or from God's law, i.e., backsliding], *that they found a plain in the land of Shinar; and they dwelt there* (Genesis 11:2).

And, behold, seven ears, withered, thin, and blasted with the east wind [cursed by the law], *sprung up after them. ... And the seven thin and ill favored kine that came up after them are seven years: and the seven empty ears blasted* [cursed] *with the east wind shall be seven years of famine* (Genesis 41:23,27).

And Moses stretched forth his rod over the land of Egypt, and the Lord brought an east wind [curse of the law] *upon the land all that day, and all that night; and when it was morning, the east wind brought the locusts* [curse] (Exodus 10:13).

As far as the east [law] *is from the west* [grace], *so far hath He removed our transgressions from us* (Psalm 103:12).

FRONT (as in **Front Yard** or **Front Porch**)—*Future or Now:* In the presence of; a prophecy of future events (that which is to come); immediate; current.

The earth also was corrupt before [in the presence of] *God, and the earth was filled with violence* (Genesis 6:11).

Write the things which thou hast seen, and the things which [presently] *are* [before, or in front of you], *and the things which shall be hereafter* (Revelation 1:19).

NORTH (on your left hand when you are facing east)— *Spiritual:* Judgment; Heaven or heavenly; spiritual warfare (as in "taking your inheritance").

The north wind driveth away rain: so doth an angry countenance [spirit judging (reproving)] *a backbiting tongue* (Proverbs 25:23).

And the word of the Lord came unto me the second time, saying, What seest thou? And I said, I see a seething pot; and the face thereof is toward the north. Then the Lord said unto me, Out of the north an evil shall break forth upon all the inhabitants of the land (Jeremiah 1:13-14).

Ye have compassed this mountain long enough: turn you northward [toward your promised inheritance] (Deuteronomy 2:3).

LEFT—*Spiritual:* Weakness (of man); God's strength or ability demonstrated through man's weakness; rejection. **Left Turn** = *Spiritual change.*

And He said unto me, My grace is sufficient for thee: for My strength is made perfect in weakness. ... For when I am weak [as man's left hand may be weak when compared to his right], *then am I strong* (2 Corinthians 12:9a, 10b).

Among all this people there were seven hundred chosen men lefthanded [spiritually empowered or gifted]; *every one could sling stones* [accurate words of knowledge] *at an hair breadth, and not miss* (Judges 20:16).

And Ehud came unto [the king]...*and Ehud said, I have a message from God unto thee... And Ehud put forth his left hand, and took the dagger from his right thigh, and thrust it into his belly* (Judges 3:20-21).

And He shall set the sheep on His right hand, but [reject] *the goats* [sinners] *on the left* (Matthew 25:33).

SOUTH (Heb.: "on your right hand when facing east")—*Natural:* World; sin; temptation; trial; flesh; corruption; deception.

So Joshua smote all the country...of the south...he left none remaining, but utterly destroyed all that breathed [flesh], *as the Lord God of Israel commanded* (Joshua 10:40).

Out of the south [flesh or world] *cometh the whirlwind: and cold* [rejection, God's judgment for sin] *out of the north* (Job 37:9).

RIGHT—*Natural:* Authority; power; the strength of man (flesh), or the power of God revealed through flesh (i.e., Christ or the Church); accepted. **Right Turn** = *Natural change.*

And if thy right eye offend thee, pluck it out [the right eye symbolizes both of the natural eyes, for one can lust with either eye], *and cast it from thee. ... And if thy right hand offend thee, cut if off* [likewise, one can steal with either hand, therefore the right hand represents both natural hands], *and cast it from thee* (Matthew 5:29-30a).

And Joseph said unto his father, Not so, my father: for this is the firstborn; put thy right hand upon his head [acknowledging or transferring authority] (Genesis 48:18).

Thy right hand, O Lord, is become glorious in power: Thy right hand [Jesus, the natural expression of the invisible God who reveals that authority and power], *O Lord, hath dashed in pieces the enemy* (Exodus 15:6).

And He shall set the sheep [those accepted of God] *on His right hand, but* [reject] *the goats* [sinners] *on the left* (Matthew 25:33).

Who [Christ] *is gone into heaven, and is on the right hand* [position of authority] *of God; angels and authorities and powers being made subject unto Him* (1 Peter 3:22).

WEST (Heb: "the region of the evening [setting] sun")—*End:* (as in "the end of the day"): Grace; death; last; conformed.

And the Lord turned a mighty strong west wind [the doctrine of grace]*, which took away the locusts* [curse]*, and cast them into the Red sea; there remained not one locust in all the coasts of Egypt* (Exodus 10:19).

As far as the east [law] *is from the west* [grace]*, so far hath He removed our transgressions from us* (Psalm 103:12).

And He said also to the people, When ye see a cloud [of glory] *rise out of the west* [grace of God]*, straightway ye say, There cometh a shower* [revival]*; and so it is* (Luke 12:54).

5

Metals

BRASS—*Word:* Word of God or man; judgment; hypocrisy; self-justification; fake; man's tradition.

And His feet [words] *like unto fine* [purified] *brass, as if they burned in a furnace; and His voice as the sound of many waters* (Revelation 1:15).

Though I speak with the tongues of men and of angels, and have not charity, I am become as sounding brass, or a tinkling cymbal (1 Corinthians 13:1).

Instead of which king Rehoboam made shields of brass [in place of gold], *and committed them to the hands of the chief of the guard, that kept the entrance of the king's house* (2 Chronicles 12:10).

Above all, taking the [gold] *shield of faith* [not the brass shield of self-justification], *wherewith ye shall be able to quench all the fiery darts of the wicked* (Ephesians 6:16).

Because I knew that thou art obstinate, and thy neck is an iron sinew [stubborn self-will], *and thy brow brass* [brazen, rude, etc.] (Isaiah 48:4).

GOLD—*Glory or wisdom:* Truth; something precious; righteousness; glory of God; self-glorification.

Then Asa brought out silver and gold out of the treasures of the house of the Lord (2 Chronicles 16:2a).

In whom are hid all the treasures of wisdom [gold] *and knowledge* [silver] (Colossians 2:3).

For if there come unto your assembly a man with a gold ring, in goodly apparel, and there come in also a poor man in vile raiment; and ye have respect to him that [glorifies himself with gold and] *weareth the gay clothing...Are ye not then partial in yourselves, and are become judges of evil thoughts?* (James 2:2-4)

IRON—*Strength:* Powerful; invincible; stronghold; stubborn.

And the fourth kingdom shall be strong as iron: forasmuch as iron breaketh in pieces and subdueth all things (Daniel 2:40a).

Because I knew that thou art obstinate [stubborn], *and thy neck is an iron sinew* [self-will], *and thy brow brass* (Isaiah 48:4).

Therefore shalt thou serve thine enemies which the Lord shall send against thee...and He shall put a yoke of iron [curse-bondage] *upon thy neck, until He have destroyed thee* (Deuteronomy 28:48).

LEAD—*Weight:* Wickedness; sin; burden (the cares of the world); judgment; fool or foolishness.

And he said, This is wickedness...and he cast the weight of lead upon the mouth thereof (Zechariah 5:8).

Thou didst blow with Thy wind, the sea covered them: they sank as lead in the mighty waters (Exodus 15:10).

A stone [or lead] is heavy, and the sand weighty; but a fool's wrath is heavier than them both (Proverbs 27:3).

Wherefore seeing we also are compassed about with so great a cloud of witnesses, let us lay aside every weight, and the sin which doth so easily beset us, and let us run with patience the race that is set before us (Hebrews 12:1).

SILVER—*Knowledge:* **Knowledge of God** = *Redemption.* **Knowledge of the World** = *Idolatry;* spiritual adultery. **Silver Coins** = *Revelation knowledge.*

Yea, if thou criest after knowledge, and liftest up thy voice for understanding; if thou seekest her as silver, and searchest for her as for hid treasures [revelation knowledge] (Proverbs 2:3-4).

And this is life eternal [redemption], *that they might know Thee the only true God, and Jesus Christ, whom Thou hast sent* (John 17:3).

For a certain man named Demetrius, a silversmith, which made silver shrines for Diana, brought no small gain unto the craftsmen (Acts 19:24).

STEEL—See IRON.

TIN—*Dross:* Waste; worthless; cheap; also, purification. (For TIN ROOF, see ROOF, *Section 2.*)

And I will turn My hand upon thee, and purely purge away thy dross [sin], *and take away all thy tin* (Isaiah 1:25).

6

Numbers

ONE—*Beginning:* First—in time, rank, order, or importance; new.

In the beginning God created the heaven and the earth. ... And the evening and the morning were the first day (Genesis 1:1,5b).

And it came to pass in the six hundredth and first year, in the first month, the first day of the month, the waters were dried up from off the earth: and Noah removed the covering of the ark... (Genesis 8:13).

TWO—*Divide:* Judge; separate; discern.

And God said, Let there be a firmament in the midst of the waters, and let it divide the waters from the waters. ... And the evening and the morning were the second day (Genesis 1:6,8b).

And the king said, Divide the living child in two, and give half to the one, and half to the other. ... And all Israel heard of the judgment which the king had judged...they saw that the wisdom of God was in him, to do judgment (1 Kings 3:25,28).

THREE—*Conform:* Obey; copy; imitate; likeness; tradition.

> *And God said...let the dry land appear: and it was so. ... And God said, Let the earth bring forth grass, the herb yielding seed, and the fruit tree yielding fruit after his kind, whose seed is in itself, upon the earth: and it was so. ... And the evening and the morning were the third day* (Genesis 1:9,11,13).

> *For whom He did foreknow, He also did predestinate to be conformed to the image of His Son* (Romans 8:29a).

FOUR—*Reign:* Rule (over the world); kingdom; creation (including things in heaven and earth); world.

> *And God made two great lights; the greater light to rule the day, and the lesser light to rule the night: He made the stars also. ... And to rule over the day and over the night, and to divide the light from the darkness... And the evening and the morning were the fourth day* (Genesis 1:16,18-19).

FIVE—*Serve:* Works; service; bondage (including debt, sickness, phobias, etc.); taxes; prison; sin; motion.

> *And God said, Let the waters bring forth abundantly the moving creature that hath life, and fowl that may fly above the earth in the open firmament of heaven. ... And the evening and the morning were the fifth day* (Genesis 1:20,23).

> *Let Pharaoh do this, and let him appoint officers over the land, and take up the fifth part of the land of Egypt in the seven plenteous years* (Genesis 41:34).

> *And if a man will at all redeem ought of his tithes, he shall add thereto the fifth part thereof* (Leviticus 27:31).

Jesus answered them, Verily, verily, I say unto you, Whosoever committeth sin is the servant of sin [Compare Romans 7:5: "For when we were in the flesh, the motions of sins...did work in our members to bring forth fruit unto death."] (John 8:34).

SIX—*Image:* Man; flesh; carnal; idol; form.

And God said, Let us make man in our image, after our likeness. ... And the evening and the morning were the sixth day (Genesis 1:26a,31b).

Here is wisdom. Let him that hath understanding count the number of the beast: for it is the number of a man; and his number is Six hundred threescore and six (Revelation 13:18).

SEVEN—*Complete:* All; finished; rest.

Thus the heavens and the earth were finished, and all the host of them. ... And God blessed the seventh day, and sanctified it: because that in it He had rested from all His work which God created and made (Genesis 2:1,3).

EIGHT—*Put off (as in putting off "the old man," i.e., the works of the flesh):* Sanctify; manifest; reveal; die; death. By implication, new beginnings (the result of putting off the old life is a new life or beginning).

And he that is eight days old shall be circumcised among you, every man child in your generations [Compare Colossians 2:11: "In whom also ye are circumcised with the circumcision made without hands, in putting off the body of the sins of the flesh by the circumcision of Christ."] (Genesis 17:12a).

Now they began on the first day of the first month to sanctify, and on the eighth day of the month came they to the porch of the Lord: so they sanctified the house of the Lord in eight days... (2 Chronicles 29:17).

...In the days of Noah, while the ark was a preparing, wherein few, that is, eight souls were saved by water. The like figure whereunto even baptism doth also now save us (not the putting away of the filth of the flesh [the baptism of repentance], *but the answer of a good conscience toward God* [i.e., the putting away of the guilt of sin (see Heb. 9:14)],*) by the resurrection of Jesus Christ* (1 Peter 3:20-21).

Lie not one to another, seeing that ye have put off the old man with his deeds (Colossians 3:9).

Knowing that shortly I must put off this my tabernacle [i.e., die], *even as our Lord Jesus Christ hath shown me* (2 Peter 1:14).

NINE—*Harvest:* Fruit; fruitfulness; fruition.

And Jesus answering said, Were there not ten cleansed? but where are the nine? [the fruit, or harvest, of thanksgiving; see Heb. 13:15] (Luke 17:17)

But now being made free from sin, and become servants to God, ye have your fruit unto holiness, and the end everlasting life (Romans 6:22).

And the children of Israel again did evil in the sight of the Lord... And the Lord sold them into the hand of Jabin king of Canaan... And the children of Israel cried unto the Lord: for he had nine hundred chariots of iron; and twenty years he mightily oppressed the children of Israel [the fruit of their sin—God's harvest of judgment (See Hosea 6:10-11 and TWENTY.)] (Judges 4:1-3).

TEN—*Measure (for the purpose of accepting or rejecting that which is measured):* Try or trial; test, or to be tested; temptation.

Fear none of those things which thou shalt suffer: behold, the devil shall cast some of you into prison, that ye may be tried; and ye shall have tribulation ten days (Revelation 2:10a).

...Thou art weighed in the balances [tried], *and art found wanting* [rejected] (Daniel 5:27).

NOTE: The meanings of the numbers from 11 through 19 are antonyms of the numbers 1 through 9. (In other words, they are the reverse or the result of the application of the base numbers, 1 through 9.) For example, 3 means to *conform*. The opposite of conforming and the result of forced conformity is rebellion. Therefore 13 means to *rebel*. (See THREE and THIRTEEN.)

When a base number is multiplied by 10, to obtain the meaning couple the key word of the base number with the thought of acceptance or rejection. For example, the date, 5/5/50 means "service accepted" (or "rejected," as the case may be); 5 means to serve, 10 means to *measure* for the purpose of accepting or rejecting—therefore 5 times 10 equals "service accepted/rejected." (See both the example below and the entry TWENTY.)

Then came Peter to Him, and said, Lord, how oft shall my brother sin against me, and I forgive him? till seven times [completely]? *Jesus saith unto him, I say not unto thee, Until seven times: but, Until seventy times seven* [both ***completely forgive*** (seven) the offense and ***completely*** *accept* (seven times ten) the offender!] (Matthew 18:21-22; see also Mt. 18:23-35).

ELEVEN—*End:* Finish; last; stop.

And when they came that were hired about the eleventh hour, they received every man a penny. ... Saying, These last have wrought but one hour, and thou hast made them equal unto us, which have borne the burden and heat of the day (Matthew 20:9,12).

TWELVE—*Joined:* United; govern; government; oversight. (Government is the means by which people are united into common purposes and goals.)

Then He called His twelve disciples together [joined or united them], *and gave them power and authority over all devils, and to cure diseases. And He sent them to preach the kingdom* [government] *of God, and to heal the sick* (Luke 9:1-2).

That ye may eat and drink at My table in My kingdom, and sit on thrones judging the twelve tribes of Israel (Luke 22:30).

Now I beseech you, brethren, by the name of our Lord Jesus Christ, that ye all speak the same thing, and that there be no divisions among you; but that ye be perfectly joined together in the same mind and in the same judgment [See Hebrews 13:17.] (1 Corinthians 1:10).

THIRTEEN—*Rebel:* Rebellion; revolution; rejection.

Twelve years they [by force] *served Chedorlaomer, and in the thirteenth year they rebelled* (Genesis 14:4).

FOURTEEN—*Double:* Recreate; reproduce; disciple; servant; bond slave (employee).

And at that time Solomon held a feast...before the Lord our God, seven days and seven days, even fourteen days (1 Kings 8:65).

FIFTEEN—*Free:* Grace; liberty; sin covered; honor.

And I will add unto thy days fifteen years; and I will deliver thee and this city out of the hand of the king of Assyria (2 Kings 20:6a).

So I bought her [Gomer, Hosea's adulterous wife] *to me for fifteen pieces of silver* (Hosea 3:2a).

Fifteen cubits upward did the waters prevail; and the mountains were covered (Genesis 7:20).

SIXTEEN—*Spirit:* Free spirited; without boundaries; without limitation; without law (and therefore without sin [See Romans 4:15.]); salvation.

Wherefore I pray you to take some meat: for this is for your health: for there shall not an hair fall from the head of any of you. ... And we were in all in the ship two hundred three-score and sixteen souls. And...they lightened the ship, and cast out the wheat into the sea (Acts 27:34,37-38).

SEVENTEEN—*Incomplete:* Immature; undeveloped; unfinished; childish; naive; a babe in Christ.

These are the generations of Jacob. Joseph, being seventeen years old, was feeding the flock with his brethren; and the lad was with the sons of Bilhah (Genesis 37:2a).

And I bought the field...and weighed him the money, even seventeen shekels of silver. ... For thus saith the Lord of hosts, the God of Israel; Houses and fields and vineyards shall be possessed again in this land (Jeremiah 32:9,15).

EIGHTEEN—*Put on:* Judgment; destruction; captivity; overcome; put on (the Spirit of) Christ.

And the anger of the Lord was hot against Israel, and He sold them into the hands of the Philistines…. And that year they vexed and oppressed the children of Israel: eighteen years (Judges 10:7-8a).

Or those eighteen, upon whom the tower in Siloam fell, and slew them, think ye that they were sinners above all men that dwelt in Jerusalem? (Luke 13:4)

And, behold, there was a woman which had a spirit of infirmity eighteen years, and was bowed together, and could in no wise lift up herself. … And ought not this woman, being a daughter of Abraham, whom Satan hath bound [put his bondage on, i.e., overcome], *lo, these eighteen years, be loosed from this bond on the Sabbath day?* (Luke 13:11,16)

NINETEEN—*Barren:* Ashamed; repentant; selflessness; without self-righteousness.

And Joab returned from following Abner: and when he had gathered all the people together, there lacked of David's servants nineteen men and Asahel (2 Samuel 2:30).

What fruit had ye then in those things whereof ye are now ashamed? for the end of those things is death (Romans 6:21).

TWENTY—*Holy:* Tried and approved (or *unholy:* tried and found wanting). **Two** = *Separated.* **Ten** = *Measured.* (See TWO and TEN.)

And round about the throne were four and twenty seats: and upon the seats I saw four and twenty elders sitting [holy elders in authority], *clothed in white raiment; and they had on their heads crowns of gold* (Revelation 4:4).

HUNDRED—*Fullness:* Full measure; full recompense; full reward, etc.

Then Isaac sowed in that land, and received in the same year an hundredfold [full harvest]: *and the Lord blessed him* (Genesis 26:12).

But he shall receive an hundredfold [full recompense] *now in this time, houses, and brethren, and sisters, and mothers, and children, and lands, with persecutions; and in the world to come eternal life* (Mark 10:30).

THOUSAND—*Maturity:* Full stature; mature service; mature judgment, etc.

And they commanded the people, saying, When ye see the ark of the covenant of the Lord your God...then ye shall remove from your place, and go after it. Yet there shall be a space between you and it, about two thousand cubits by measure [follow using mature judgment (Compare Ephesians 5:17: "Wherefore be ye not unwise, but understanding what the will of the Lord is.")]: *come not near unto it, that ye may know the way by which ye must go: for ye have not passed this way heretofore* (Joshua 3:3-4).

...And he was armed with a coat of mail; and the weight of the coat was five thousand [mature service] *shekels of brass. ... And Saul said to David, Thou art not able to go against this Philistine to fight with him: for thou art but a youth, and he a man of war* [mature] *from his youth* (1 Samuel 17:5,33).

Till we all come in the unity of the faith, and of the knowledge of the Son of God, unto a perfect [mature] *man, unto the measure of the stature of the fullness of Christ* (Ephesians 4:13).

7

People/Relatives/Trades

BABY—*New:* Beginning; new idea; new work (church); dependant; helpless; innocent; sin; natural baby.

And I, brethren, could not speak unto you as unto spiritual, but as unto carnal, even as unto babes in Christ (1 Corinthians 3:1).

As newborn babes, desire the sincere milk of the word, that ye may grow thereby (1 Peter 2:2).

Behold, I will do a new thing; now it shall spring forth [new birth]; *shall ye not know it? I will even make a way in the wilderness, and rivers in the desert* (Isaiah 43:19).

But every man is tempted, when he is drawn away of his own lust, and enticed. Then when lust hath conceived, it bringeth forth sin: and sin, when it is finished, bringeth forth death (James 1:14-15).

BAKER—*Instigator:* One who cooks up (and serves) ideas; originator; Christ; satan; minister; self. (See OVEN, *Section 9.*)

They are all adulterers, as an oven heated by the baker [inflamed by lust, tempted by satan], *who ceaseth from raising after he hath kneaded the dough, until it be leavened* (Hosea 7:4).

For they have made ready their heart like an oven, whiles they lie in wait: their baker [minister] *sleepeth all the night; in the morning it burneth as a flaming fire* (Hosea 7:6).

BLACK MAN—If a **stranger**, see BLACK, *Section 3,* and MAN (stranger); If **known**, see specific person: BROTHER, CARPENTER, FRIEND, etc.

BRIDE (as participating in a marriage ceremony)— *Church:* Covenant (good or evil). **Groom** = *Christ;* natural marriage when naturally interpreted. (See MARRIAGE, *Section 9.*)

For as a young man marrieth a virgin, so shall thy sons marry thee: and as the bridegroom rejoiceth over the bride, so shall thy God rejoice over thee [the Church] (Isaiah 62:5).

For this cause shall a man leave his father and mother, and shall be joined unto his wife, and they two shall be one flesh. This is a great mystery: but I speak concerning Christ and the church (Ephesians 5:31-32).

Be ye not unequally yoked together with unbelievers: for what fellowship hath righteousness with unrighteousness? and what communion hath light with darkness? (2 Corinthians 6:14)

BROTHER—*Self:* Spiritual or natural brother; someone he reminds you of. (See FRIEND.)

But why dost thou judge thy brother? or why dost thou set at nought thy brother? (Romans 14:10a)

Therefore thou art inexcusable, O man, whosoever thou art that judgest: for wherein thou judgest another [your brother], *thou condemnest thyself; for thou that judgest doest the same things* (Romans 2:1).

Remember them that are in bonds, as bound with them; and them which suffer adversity, as being yourselves also in the body (Hebrews 13:3).

BROTHER-IN-LAW—*Partiality or adversary:* Fellow minister; someone he reminds you of (see FRIEND); problem relationship; partner; oneself, he may represent himself.

I charge thee before God, and the Lord Jesus Christ, and the elect angels, that thou observe these things without preferring one before another, doing nothing by partiality (1 Timothy 5:21).

And Esther [the king's wife] *said, The adversary and enemy is this wicked Haman* [close friend of the king (as a wife's husband's brother is a friend of her husband, but not necessarily a friend to her)] (Esther 7:6a).

CARPENTER—*Builder:* Preacher; evangelist; laborer (good or evil); Christ.

Unto carpenters, and builders, and masons, and to buy timber and hewn stone to repair [edify] *the house* [of God] (2 Kings 22:6).

So the carpenter encouraged the goldsmith, and he that smootheth with the hammer him that smote the anvil...and he fastened it [the idol] *with nails, that it should not be moved* (Isaiah 41:7).

Is not this [Jesus] *the carpenter, the son of Mary...and they were offended at Him* (Mark 6:3).

CARTOON CHARACTER—*Person:* One who is like or is acting in the same way as the cartoon character. For example, **Goofy** = *Foolish:* dumb actions. **Mickey Mouse** = *Sensitive hearing* (because of his large ears): insignificant (as in "you mean that mickey mouse thing?").

> *Then said all the trees* [people] *unto the bramble* [bad, unsuitable, corrupt person], *Come thou, and reign over us* (Judges 9:14).

CLOWN—*Fool:* Foolish works of the flesh; the "old man"; childish; mischief. (See DRUNK.)

> *The heart of the wise is in the house of mourning; but the heart of fools* [clowns] *is in the house of mirth* (Ecclesiastes 7:4).

> *It is as sport to a fool to do mischief* (Proverbs 10:23a).

DAUGHTER—See ONE'S CHILDREN.

DOCTOR—*Healer:* Authority; Christ; preacher; medical doctor.

> *When Jesus heard it, He saith unto them, They that are whole have no need of the physician, but they that are sick: I came not to call the righteous, but sinners to repentance* (Mark 2:17).

> *And had suffered many things of many physicians, and had spent all that she had, and was nothing bettered, but rather grew worse* (Mark 5:26).

> *And Asa in the thirty and ninth year of his reign was diseased in his feet, until his disease was exceeding great: yet in his disease he sought not to the Lord, but to the physicians* [he would not repent, but died under the chastening

hand of God (See 1 Corinthians 11:30-32.)] (2 Chronicles 16:12).

DRIVER—*Control:* Self; Christ; pastor; teacher; satan; the emphasis may be on the nature of the driver (careless, careful, frantic, confident, selfish, rude, kind, etc.). **Passenger** = *Self:* Church member; family member. When a school bus driver represents a teacher, his passengers usually represent his students. (See FRIEND.)

And the watchman told, saying...and the driving is like the driving of Jehu the son of Nimshi; for he driveth furiously (2 Kings 9:20).

DRUNK—*Influenced:* Under a spell (i.e., under the influence of the Holy Spirit or a demonic spirit, such as witchcraft); controlled; addicted; fool; unchangeable; stubborn; rebellious; selfish; self-indulging; proud; conceited; arrogant; boastful.

And be not drunk with [natural] *wine, wherein is excess; but be filled with the Spirit* [new wine, scc Acts 2:13-18] (Ephesians 5:18).

And take heed to yourselves, lest at any time your hearts be overcharged with surfeiting, and drunkenness, and cares of this life, and so that day come upon you unawares (Luke 21:34).

And they shall say unto the elders of his city, This our son is stubborn and rebellious, he will not obey our voice; he is a glutton, and a drunkard (Deuteronomy 21:20).

A wise man feareth, and departeth from evil: but the fool [or drunk] *rageth, and is confident* [arrogant and boastful] (Proverbs 14:16).

The way of a fool [or drunk] *is right in his own eyes: but he that hearkeneth unto counsel is wise* (Proverbs 12:15).

EMPLOYEE—*Servant:* **Fellow Employee** = *Self,* another employee (see FRIEND), or the actual employee when naturally interpreted.

Servants [or employees], *obey in all things your masters* [employers] *according to the flesh; not with eyeservice, as menpleasers; but in singleness of heart, fearing God* (Colossians 3:22).

EMPLOYER—*Authority:* Pastor; Christ; satan; someone he or she resembles, in position, action or character (see NAME, *Section 9*); actual employer when naturally interpreted.

Masters [or employers], *give unto your servants* [employees] *that which is just and equal; knowing that ye also have a Master in heaven* (Colossians 4:1).

FAMILY—*Relatives:* Spiritual family (Church) or natural family.

And the ark of God remained with the family of Obededom in his house three months. And the Lord blessed the house of Obededom, and all that he had (1 Chronicles 13:14).

Of whom the whole family [Church] *in heaven and earth is named* (Ephesians 3:15).

FARMER—*Laborer:* Preacher; pastor; Christ; minister. **Farm** = *Field of labor:* an area of ministry; the Kingdom of God; the Church. (See BARN, *Section 2*, and GARDENING, *Section 9*.)

The sower [farmer] *soweth the word* (Mark 4:14).

Now he that ministereth seed to the sower both minister bread for your food, and multiply your seed sown, and increase the fruits of your righteousness (2 Corinthians 9:10).

FATHER—*Authority:* God; author; originator; source; inheritance; tradition; custom; satan; natural father.

Have we not all one father? hath not one God created us? (Malachi 2:10a)

Honor thy father and mother; which is the first commandment with promise (Ephesians 6:2).

I seek not yours, but you: for the children ought not to lay up for the parents, but the parents for the children (2 Corinthians 12:14b).

And Adah bare Jabal: he was the father of such as dwell in tents, and of such as have cattle. And his brother's name was Jubal: he was the father of all such as handle the harp and organ (Genesis 4:20-21).

Ye are of your father the devil, and the lusts of your father ye will do. He was a murderer from the beginning, and abode not in the truth, because there is no truth in him. When he speaketh a lie, he speaketh of his own: for he is a liar, and the father [originator] *of it* (John 8:44).

FATHER-IN-LAW—*Law:* Authoritative relationship based upon law (as in "Moses' Law or church government"); legalism; problem (authoritative) relationship; he may represent himself.

And Moses' father-in-law said unto him, The thing that thou doest is not good (Exodus 18:17).

FOREIGNER—*Alien:* Not of God; of the flesh; demonic; not of this world (therefore heavenly). (See NATION.)

Our inheritance is turned to strangers [or foreigners], *our houses to aliens* (Lamentations 5:2).

As cold waters to a thirsty soul, so is good news from a far country [the Kingdom of Heaven] (Proverbs 25:25).

FRIEND—*Self:* The character or circumstance of one's friend reveals something about oneself. Sometimes one friend represents another (look for another with the same name, initials, hair color, job, or trade, or one with similar traits, character, talents, personality, features, circumstances, etc. (See NAME, *Section 9*); actual friend when naturally interpreted.

And he [King Saul] *took Agag the king of the Amalekites alive* [thus symbolically sparing himself (his own flesh)], *and utterly destroyed all the people with the edge of the sword* (1 Samuel 15:8).

GARDENER—See FARMER.

GIANT—*Strongman:* Champion; stronghold; challenge; obstacle; trouble; spiritual warfare; one's own fleshly nature (to be overcome).

The land, through which we have gone to search it, is a land that eateth up the inhabitants thereof; and all the people that we saw in it are men of a great stature. And there we saw the giants, the sons of Anak...and we were in our own sight as grasshoppers, and so we were in their sight (Numbers 13:32b-33).

GOVERNOR—*Rule:* Christ; person in charge (good or bad).

And if ye offer the blind for sacrifice [to God], *is it not evil?...offer it now unto thy governor; will he be pleased with thee, or accept thy person? saith the Lord of hosts* (Malachi 1:8).

GRANDCHILD—*Heir:* Oneself; inherited blessing or iniquity; one's spiritual legacy; actual grandchild when naturally interpreted. (See GRANDMOTHER.)

When I call to remembrance the unfeigned faith that is in thee, which dwelt first in thy grandmother Lois, and thy mother Eunice; and I am persuaded that in thee also (2 Timothy 1:5).

Keeping mercy for thousands, forgiving iniquity and transgression and sin, and that will by no means clear the guilty; visiting the iniquity of the fathers upon the children, and upon the children's children, unto the third and to the fourth generation (Exodus 34:7).

So these nations feared the Lord, and served their graven images, both their children, and their children's children... (2 Kings 17:41).

GRANDMOTHER (or Grandfather)—*Past:* Spiritual inheritance (good or evil). (See ANTIQUES, *Section 9,* and HOUSE, *Section 2.*) Self-examination for inherited traits, faults, or sins.

When I call to remembrance the unfeigned faith that is in thee, which dwelt first in thy grandmother Lois, and thy mother Eunice; and I am persuaded that in thee also (2 Timothy 1:5).

A good man leaveth an inheritance to his children's children (Proverbs 13:22a).

And they that are left of you shall pine away in their iniquity in your enemies' lands; and also in the iniquities of their fathers shall they pine away with them. If they shall confess their iniquity, and the iniquity of their fathers…. Then will I remember My covenant…with Abraham…and I will remember the land (Leviticus 26:39-40,42).

GROOM—See BRIDE, *Section 7*, and MARRIAGE, *Section 9.*

HARLOT—*Seduction:* The worldly church; adultery; fornication; temptation; snare; unclean person; stubborn. (See SEX, *Section 9.*)

And upon her forehead was a name written, MYSTERY [RELIGION], BABYLON THE GREAT, THE MOTHER OF HARLOTS AND ABOMINATIONS OF THE EARTH (Revelation 17:5).

And I find more bitter than death the woman, whose heart is snares and nets, and her hands as bands: whoso pleaseth God shall escape from her; but the sinner shall be taken by her (Ecclesiastes 7:26).

Therefore the showers have been withholden, and there hath been no latter rain; and thou hadst a whore's forehead, thou refusedst to be ashamed (Jeremiah 3:3).

HUSBAND—*Authority:* God or Christ; a divorcee's first husband sometimes represents "the world" (her bondage to sin before she was saved), natural husband; also, satan.

Unto the woman He said…thy desire shall be to thy husband, and he shall rule over thee (Genesis 3:16).

For thy Maker is thine husband; the Lord of hosts is His name…The God of the whole earth shall He be called (Isaiah 54:5).

Surely as a wife treacherously departeth from her husband, so have ye dealt treacherously with me, O house of Israel [or Church], *saith the Lord* (Jeremiah 3:20).

INDIAN—*First:* Flesh (as in "the old man"); firstborn; chief; fierce; savvy; native.

Lie not one to another, seeing that ye have put off the old man with his deeds (Colossians 3:9).

Reuben, thou art my firstborn, my might, and the beginning of my strength, the excellency of dignity, and the excellency of power [as Christ is the firstborn among many brethren] (Genesis 49:3).

Then pleased it the apostles and elders, with the whole church, to send chosen men of their own company to Antioch with Paul and Barnabas; namely, Judas surnamed Barsabas, and Silas, chief men among the brethren (Acts 15:22).

JUDGE—*Authority:* God; conscience. **Evil Judge** = *satan;* evil authority. (See COURTHOUSE, *Section 2*, and LAWYER, *Section 7*.)

But God is the judge: he putteth down one, and setteth up another (Psalm 75:7).

Grudge not one against another, brethren, lest ye be condemned: behold, the judge standeth before the door (James 5:9).

Shall the throne of iniquity [authority of satan, an evil judge] *have fellowship with thee, which frameth mischief by a law?* (Psalm 94:20)

For if we would judge ourselves [obey our conscience], *we should not be judged* (1 Corinthians 11:31).

LAWYER—*Advocate:* Christ; a legalistic minister. **Crooked Lawyer** = *The devil's advocate* (the accuser of the brethren). (See COURTHOUSE, *Section 2,* and JUDGE, *Section 7.*)

My little children, these things write I unto you, that ye sin not. And if any man sin, we have an advocate [lawyer] with the Father, Jesus Christ the righteous (1 John 2:1).

And He said, Woe unto you also, ye lawyers! for ye lade men with burdens grievous to be borne, and ye yourselves touch not the burdens with one of your fingers (Luke 11:46).

And I heard a loud voice saying in heaven, Now is come salvation, and strength, and the kingdom of our God, and the power of His Christ: for the accuser [evil, crooked, lying advocate] of our brethren is cast down, which accused them before our God day and night (Revelation 12:10).

MAN (stranger) —*Angel, oneself, or a demon:* God's messenger (angel); person with evil intent; danger. **Kind stranger** = *Jesus;* a minister of mercy; helper. (See FRIEND.) **White-headed stranger** = *Wisdom* (see NAME, Section 9).

And when they were departed, behold, the angel [a strange man, or messenger] of the Lord appeareth to Joseph in a dream, saying, Arise, and take the young child and His mother, and flee into Egypt...for Herod will seek the young child to destroy Him (Matthew 2:13).

Be not forgetful to entertain [also hear, or heed] strangers: for thereby some have entertained angels unawares (Hebrews 13:2).

But a certain Samaritan, as he journeyed, came where he was: and when he saw him, he had compassion on him (Luke 10:33).

MECHANIC—*Minister:* Christ; prophet; pastor; counselor; need for adjustment in theology, attitude, relationship, etc. **Mechanic's Tools** = *Word of God;* gifts of the Spirit; wisdom and knowledge.

And I have filled him with the spirit of God, in wisdom, and in understanding, and in knowledge, and in all manner of workmanship [to manufacture and repair], *to devise cunning works, to work in gold* [to glorify God], *and in silver* [redemption through the knowledge of God], *and in brass* [the Word of God] (Exodus 31:3-4).

All scripture is given by inspiration of God, and is profitable for doctrine, for reproof, for correction, for instruction in righteousness (2 Timothy 3:16).

MOTHER—*Source:* Church; spiritual or natural mother; love; kindness. **Mother-in-law** = *Legalistic church;* meddler; trouble; she may represent herself. (See FATHER-IN-LAW.)

And Adam called his wife's name Eve [Heb.: "life-giver"]; *because she was the mother* [source] *of all living* (Genesis 3:20).

And of Zion [the Church] *it shall be said, This and that man was born* [again] *in her: and the highest himself shall establish her. The Lord shall count, when he writeth up the people, that this man was born* [again] *there* (Psalm 87:5-6).

OLD MAN (Unknown)—*Wisdom (especially if he is white headed):* Carnal (as in "put off the old man"); weak; fool (as in "there's no fool like an old fool").

And Elihu...answered and said, I am young, and ye are very old; wherefore I was afraid, and durst not show you mine opinion. I said, Days should speak, and multitude of years should teach wisdom (Job 32:6-7).

Great men are not always wise: neither do the aged understand judgment (Job 32:9).

The hoary [white or gray] *head is a crown of glory, if it be found in the way of righteousness* (Proverbs 16:31).

ONE'S CHILDREN—*Oneself or themselves:* Character or behavior reveals something about oneself (or something about one's own child if the dream is to be naturally interpreted). Sometimes children gathered together from different families from one's own Church represent the Church members.

Behold, every one that useth proverbs shall use this proverb against thee, saying, As is the mother, so is her daughter [or as is the daughter, so is her mother; as is the father, so is his son, etc.] (Ezekiel 16:44).

And I will give children to be their princes, and babes shall rule over them. ... As for My people, children are their oppressors, and women rule over them (Isaiah 3:4,12a).

PASSENGER—See DRIVER.

PASTOR—See PREACHER.

PILOT—See DRIVER.

POLICE—*Authority:* Natural (civil) or spiritual authority (pastors, etc.), good or evil; protection; angels or demons; an enforcer of a curse of the law (because of transgression or an evil covenant).

Let every soul be subject unto the higher powers [police, etc]. *For there is no power but of God: the powers that be are ordained of God. ... For he is the minister of God to thee for good. But if thou do that which is evil, be afraid; for he beareth not the sword in vain: for he is the minister of God, a revenger to execute wrath upon him that doeth evil* (Romans 13:1,4).

And when they [persecute you and] *bring you unto the synagogues* [churches], *and unto magistrates* [civil courts], *and powers* [natural or spiritual], *take ye no thought how or what thing ye shall answer, or what ye shall say* (Luke 12:11).

Shall the throne of iniquity [authority of satan] *have fellowship with thee, which frameth mischief by a law?* (Psalm 94:20)

And of the angels He saith, Who maketh His angels spirits, and His ministers a flame of fire. ... Are they not all ministering spirits [as public servants, or police], *sent forth to minister for them who shall be heirs of salvation?* (Hebrews 1:7,14)

PREACHER—*Messenger:* God's representative; spiritual authority (good or evil, because he can also represent satan); deception. **Pastor's Wife** = *Church.*

And I will give you pastors [preachers and teachers] *according to mine heart, which shall feed you with knowledge and understanding* (Jeremiah 3:15).

Woe be unto the pastors that destroy and scatter the sheep of my pasture! saith the Lord (Jeremiah 23:1).

For such are false apostles [preachers], *deceitful workers, transforming themselves into the apostles of Christ* (2 Corinthians 11:13).

SISTER—*Self:* Spiritual sister (sister in Christ); someone she reminds you of (see NAME, *Section 9*); the Church; she may represent herself.

For whosoever shall do the will of My Father which is in heaven [the Church], *the same is My brother, and sister, and mother* (Matthew 12:50).

SISTER-IN-LAW—Someone she reminds you of or she may represent her family, herself, or the dreamer when the dreamer is female (see FRIEND). Other possibilities are: **Brother's Wife** = *Brother.* **Husband's Sister** = *Church.* **Wife's Sister** = *Wife.* (*Note:* In any case, if she is the wife of a minister, she may represent the Church.)

Thou shalt not uncover the nakedness of thy brother's wife: it is thy brother's nakedness (Leviticus 18:16).

SOLDIER—*Warfare:* Spiritual warfare; angel (protection); demon (accuser or opponent); persecution. (See GUNS/BULLETS, *Section 9.*)

And there was war in heaven: Michael and his angels fought against the dragon; and the dragon fought and his angels. ...the accuser of our brethren is cast down, which accused them before our God day and night (Revelation 12:7,10).

Thou therefore endure hardness, as a good soldier of Jesus Christ. No man that warreth entangleth himself with the affairs of this life; that he may please him who hath chosen him to be a soldier (2 Timothy 2:3-4).

The words of his mouth were smoother than butter, but war was in his heart: his words were softer than oil, yet were they drawn swords (Psalm 55:21).

SON—See ONE'S CHILDREN.

THIEF—*Hidden:* Deceiver; deception; fraud; destruction; satan; evil intent; works of the flesh; unexpected lost.

The thief's victim = *One who is a victim of false doctrine* (as in truth lost through tradition or philosophy); lost of liberty, or even salvation; also, temptation; unaware; secret; covert operation; God's judgment (curse) on the wicked.

The thief cometh not, but for to steal, and to kill, and to destroy (John 10:10a).

Beware lest any man [thief] *spoil* [rob] *you* [of the truth] *through philosophy and vain deceit, after the tradition of men, after the rudiments of the world, and not after Christ* (Colossians 2:8).

Whoso is partner with a thief hateth his own soul: he heareth cursing, and bewrayeth it not (Proverbs 29:24).

For yourselves know perfectly that the day of the Lord so cometh as a thief in the night. ... But ye, brethren, are not in darkness, that that day should overtake you as a thief (1 Thessalonians 5:2,4).

WARRIOR—See SOLDIER.

WIFE—*Covenant:* Joined; job; business; hobby; Church; dedicated involvement in any activity, such as a job, business, Church, etc.; help; her husband's own person; she may represent herself. (See MARRIAGE, *Section 9.*)

Which things are an allegory: for these [two wives of Abraham] *are the two covenants* (Galatians 4:24a).

For the husband is the head of the wife, even as Christ is the head of the church: and He is the savior of the body. ... This is a great mystery: but I speak concerning Christ and the church (Ephesians 5:23,32).

But he that is married [to his wife, job, business, hobby, etc.] *careth for the things that are of the world, how he may please his wife* [his own flesh] (1 Corinthians 7:33).

WITCH—*Witchcraft:* Control; evil influence; evil intent; seduction; non-submissive wife; rebellion; slander; gossip; worldly church; evil spirit.

For rebellion is as the sin of witchcraft (1 Samuel 15:23a).

But there was none like unto Ahab, which did sell himself to work wickedness in the sight of the Lord, whom [the witch] *Jezebel his wife stirred up* [or controlled] (1 Kings 21:25).

Notwithstanding I have a few things against thee, because thou sufferest that woman Jezebel, which calleth herself a prophetess, to teach and to seduce My servants to commit fornication, and to eat things sacrificed unto idols (Revelation 2:20).

WOMAN (stranger)—*Spirit:* Seducing spirit; temptation; deception; witchcraft; God's messenger (angel); one's own self. (See HARLOT, *Section 7,* and NAME, *Section 9.*)

To deliver thee from the strange woman, even from the stranger which flattereth with her words (Proverbs 2:16).

It is like leaven, which a woman took and hid in three measures of meal, till the whole was leavened (Luke 13:21).

For a whore is a deep ditch; and a strange woman is a narrow pit (Proverbs 23:27).

8

Vehicles and Parts

AIRPLANE—*Person or Work:* Church (large airplane, such as a passenger plane); travel. **Small Airplane** = *A person or personal ministry;* oversight. **Flying or Soaring** = *Moved by the Spirit;* ministering in the gifts of the Spirit. **Flying Near Electrical Power Lines** = *Danger;* caution; need for much prayer. **Flying Too Low** = *Insufficient power (prayer) or preparation (training);* not following (being led by) the Spirit. **Airplane Crash** = *Failure;* church split (the survivors are those remaining after the split); personal disaster (i.e., a failed marriage, business venture, etc.). (See FALLING, *Section 9;* for PILOT see DRIVER, *Section 7.*)

> *And He rode upon a cherub, and did fly: yea, He did fly upon the wings of the wind* (Psalm 18:10).

> *And when they were come up out of the water, the Spirit of the Lord caught away Philip, that the eunuch saw him no more* (Acts 8:39a).

JET—*Ministry or Minister:* Powerful; fast. **Passenger Jet** = *Church.* **Fighter** = *Individual person or ministry.*

And a certain Jew named Apollos...an eloquent man, and mighty in the scriptures, came to Ephesus (Acts 18:24).

AUTOMOBILE—*Life:* Person; ministry. **New Car** = *New ministry or new way of life.* **Automobile Breakdown** = *Problem;* sickness; trouble; opposition; hinderance (to one's ministry, career, livelihood, etc.). **Limousine** = *Important;* pride. (See VAN.)

And he made him to ride in the second chariot [limousine] *which he had; and they cried before him, Bow the knee: and he made him ruler over all the land of Egypt* (Genesis 41:43).

And he said, Come with me, and see my zeal for the Lord. So they made him ride in his chariot (2 Kings 10:16).

Wherefore we would have come unto you, even I Paul, once and again; but Satan hindered us (1 Thessalonians 2:18).

CONVERTIBLE (with the top up)—*Covered:* The emphasis is on the covering of the auto owner or driver's life (i.e., spirit, attitude, covenant, etc.).

CONVERTIBLE (with the top down)—*Uncovered:* Everything revealed; open, nothing hidden; a self-righteous or unsaved person; "Living in the fast lane"; not submitted to authority; pride; sin or evil exposed. (See MOTORCYCLE.)

And herein do I exercise myself, to have always a conscience void of offense toward God, and toward men (Acts 24:16).

And he drank of the wine, and was drunken; and he was uncovered within his tent (Genesis 9:21).

But every woman that prayeth or prophesieth with her head uncovered [not under or submitted to authority, including obedience to (the authority of) her conscience] *dishonoreth her head: for that is even all one as if she were shaven* (1 Corinthians 11:5).

Woe to the rebellious children, saith the Lord, that take counsel, but not of Me; and that cover with a covering, but not of My spirit, that they may add sin to sin (Isaiah 30:1).

AUTO JUNKYARD—*Ruined:* Waste; wrecked; lost souls; corruption. (See GARBAGE DUMP, *Section 9.*)

The wicked shall be turned into hell [the junkyard of wrecked lives], *and all the nations that forget God* (Psalm 9:17).

But he knoweth not that the dead are there; and that her [a harlot's] *guests are in the depths of hell* (Proverbs 9:18).

Therefore hell hath enlarged herself, and opened her mouth without measure: and their glory, and their multitude, and their pomp, and he that rejoiceth, shall descend into it (Isaiah 5:14).

AUTO WRECK—*Strife:* Contention; conflict; confrontation; calamity; offense; mistake or sin in ministry (as in "failure to maintain right of way"). (See BOAT.)

The chariots [automobiles, i.e., people] *shall rage in the streets, they shall jostle one against another in the broad ways* [worldly churches or paths of unrighteousness]: *they shall seem like torches, they shall run like the lightnings* (Nahum 2:4).

BATTERY—*Power:* Strength; prayer; motivation; weak; without spiritual power.

But ye, beloved, building [charging] *up yourselves on your most holy faith, praying in the Holy Ghost* (Jude 1:20).

BICYCLE—*Works:* Works of the flesh (i.e., not of faith); legalism; self-righteousness; working out life's difficulties (as in riding uphill or in sand or mud); messenger (as in "a paper delivery boy"); **Bicycle Built for Two (or with child seat)** = *Family;* more than one person involved.

Christ is become of no effect unto you, whosoever of you are justified by the law [works]; *ye are fallen from grace* (Galatians 5:4).

Now the works of the flesh are manifest, which are these; Adultery, fornication, uncleanness, lasciviousness (Galatians 5:19).

BLIMP—*Weak:* Moved by every wind; wimp; controlled; powerless; aimless; puffed up.

That we henceforth be no more children, tossed to and fro, and carried about with every wind of doctrine, by the sleight of men, and cunning craftiness, whereby they lie in wait to deceive (Ephesians 4:14).

BOAT—*Support:* Life; person; recreation; spare time. **Large Ship** = *The Church.* **Small Boat** = *Personal ministry.* **Sailboat** = *Moved by the Spirit.* **Powerboat** = *Powerful ministry or fast progress.* **Battleship** = *Spiritual warfare;* rescue. **Shipwreck** = *Apostasy;* church split.

A window [revelation knowledge] *shalt thou make to the ark* [Church], *and in a cubit shalt thou finish it above; and the door* [Christ] *of the ark shalt thou set in the side thereof; with lower* [body], *second* [soul], *and third* [spirit] *stories shalt thou make it* (Genesis 6:16).

Now it came to pass on a certain day, that He went into a ship with His disciples: and He said unto them, Let us go over unto the other side of the lake. And they launched forth. But as they sailed He fell asleep: and there came down a storm of wind on the lake; and they were filled with water [despair], *and were in jeopardy* [See STORM.] (Luke 8:22-23).

Holding faith, and a good conscience; which some having put away concerning faith have made shipwreck (1 Timothy 1:19).

BRAKES—*Stop:* Hindrance; resist; wait. **Brakes Fail =** *Overcome;* not able to discontinue a bad habit or change a tradition; no resistance to temptation.

Now when they had gone throughout Phrygia and the region of Galatia, and were forbidden of the Holy Ghost to preach the word in Asia, after they were come to Mysia, they assayed to go into Bithynia: but the Spirit suffered them not (Acts 16:6-7).

Having eyes full of adultery, and that cannot cease from sin... [brakes fail] (2 Peter 2:14).

BUS—*Church:* **School Bus =** *Teaching or youth ministry;* learning; working together. **Passenger or Tour Bus =** *Sojourners;* Christians; sight-seers. (See PASSENGER, Section 7.)

And Elisha came again to Gilgal...and the sons of the prophets were sitting before him [as he taught them]: *and he said unto his servant, Set on the great pot, and seethe pottage for the sons of the prophets* (2 Kings 4:38).

And the things that thou hast heard of me among many witnesses, the same commit thou [teach] *to faithful men, who shall be able to teach others also* (2 Timothy 2:2).

By faith he sojourned in the land of promise, as in a strange country (Hebrews 11:9a).

CAR—See AUTOMOBILE.

FOUR-WHEEL DRIVE VEHICLE—See TIRES and PICKUP TRUCK.

HELICOPTER—*Ministry:* Individual; the Church; versatile. **Hovering** = *No forward motion;* stationary; lack of progress.

Preach the word; be instant in season, out of season; reprove, rebuke, exhort (2 Timothy 4:2a).

MOTOR—*Power:* Motive; motivation; anointing.

How God anointed Jesus of Nazareth with the Holy Ghost and with power: who went about doing good, and healing all that were oppressed of the devil; for God was with Him (Acts 10:38).

MOTORCYCLE—*Individual:* Personal ministry; independence; rebellion; selfish; pride; swift progress.

But chiefly them that walk after the flesh in the lust of uncleanness, and despise government. Presumptuous are they, self-willed, they are not afraid to speak evil of dignities (2 Peter 2:10).

For rebellion is as the sin of witchcraft, and stubbornness is as iniquity and idolatry (1 Samuel 15:23a).

MOVING VAN—*Change:* Geographical move (natural or spiritual, i.e., moving from one house or place to another, or moving from one church to another, including changing denominations); relocation.

Son of man...prepare thee stuff for removing, and remove by day in their sight; and thou shalt remove from thy place to another place in their sight... (Ezekiel 12:2-3).

PICKUP TRUCK—*Work:* Personal ministry or natural work. (See AUTOMOBILE.)

And they carried the ark of God in a new cart out of the house of Abinadab: and Uzza and Ahio drave the cart (1 Chronicles 13:7).

...And when he [Jacob] saw the wagons which Joseph had sent to carry him, the spirit of Jacob their father revived [revival] (Genesis 45:27).

For every man shall bear his own burden [drive his own truck, i.e., do his own work, natural or spiritual] (Galatians 6:5).

PILOT—See DRIVER, *Section 7.*

RAFT—*Adrift:* Without direction; aimless; powerless; makeshift.

And the rest, some on boards, and some on broken pieces of the ship. And so it came to pass, that they escaped all safe to land (Acts 27:44).

That we henceforth be no more children, tossed to and fro, and carried about with every wind [or current] *of doctrine* (Ephesians 4:14a).

REARVIEW MIRROR—*Word:* **Driving Backward (using the rearview mirror)** = *Operating by the letter of the Word* (instead of by God's Spirit); legalism; looking back. (See MIRROR, *Section 9.*)

Who also hath made us able ministers of the new testament; not of the letter, but of the spirit: for the letter killeth, but the spirit giveth life (2 Corinthians 3:6).

But his [Lot's] *wife looked back from behind him* [regretting having to leave the things of this world], *and she became a pillar of salt* (Genesis 19:26).

ROLLER COASTER—*Unstable:* Emotional instability; unfaithfulness; wavering; manic-depressive; depression; trials; excitement.

Every valley shall be exalted, and every mountain and hill shall be made low: and the crooked shall be made straight, and the rough places plain [or smooth] (Isaiah 40:4).

But let him ask in faith, nothing wavering. For he that wavereth is like a wave of the sea driven with the wind and tossed. For let not that man think that he shall receive any thing of the Lord. A double minded man is unstable in all his ways (James 1:6-8).

ROWBOAT—See ROWING, *Section 9.*

SCHOOL BUS—See BUS.

SEAT BELT—*Security:* Safety; assurance. **Unfastened** = *Unsafe* (lack of prayer, commitment, attention to detail, etc.).

...Bind the sacrifice with cords [vows, commitment, etc], *even unto the horns of the altar* (Psalm 118:27).

SHIP—See BOAT.

STATION WAGON—See VAN.

TIRES—*Spirit:* Life (as in "where the rubber meets the road"); spiritual condition. **Four-Wheel Drive** = *Full ministry;* full gospel foundation. **Deflated Tire** = *Discouragement;* dismay; hindrance; lack of prayer.

And took off their chariot wheels, that they drave them heavily [discouraged them]*: so that the Egyptians said, Let us flee from the face of Israel; for the Lord fighteth for them against the Egyptians* (Exodus 14:25).

Whithersoever the spirit was to go, they went, thither was their spirit to go; and the wheels were lifted up over against them: for the spirit of the living creature was in the wheels (Ezekiel 1:20).

TRACTOR (FARM)—*Powerful Work:* Slow but powerful ministry; preaching (when plowing).

But ye shall receive power, after that the Holy Ghost is come upon you: and ye shall be witnesses unto Me...unto the uttermost part of the earth (Acts 1:8).

And with great power gave the apostles witness of the resurrection of the Lord Jesus: and great grace was upon them all (Acts 4:33).

TRACTOR TRAILER—*Large Burden:* Ministry; powerful and/or large work (truck size is often in proportion to the burden or size of the work); the Church.

And they set the ark of God upon a new cart...and Uzzah and Ahio...drave the new cart (2 Samuel 6:3).

And believers were the more added to the Lord, multitudes [large work] *both of men and women* (Acts 5:14).

TRAIN—*Continuous:* Unceasing work; the Church; connected; fast. **Train Wreck** = *Similar to* **Airplane Crash**. (See AIRPLANE, *Section 8,* and RAILROAD TRACK, *Section 9.*)

And they continued stedfastly in the apostles' doctrine and fellowship, and in breaking of bread, and in prayers (Acts 2:42).

TRANSMISSION—*Change:* Steps; change of direction, change of purpose or intensity of ministry; transformation.

> *And be not conformed to this world: but be ye transformed by the renewing of your mind* (Romans 12:2a).

TRUCK—See PICKUP TRUCK and TRACTOR TRAILER.

VAN—*Family:* Natural or church family; family ministry; fellowship.

> *For this cause I bow my knees unto the Father of our Lord Jesus Christ, of whom the whole family in heaven and earth is named* (Ephesians 3:14-15).

> *But if we walk in the light, as He is in the light, we have fellowship one with another, and the blood of Jesus Christ His Son cleanseth us from all sin* (1 John 1:7).

WHEELS—See TIRES.

9

Miscellaneous

ACID—*Bitter:* Offense; carrying a grudge; hatred; sarcasm.

For I perceive that thou art in the gall of bitterness, and in the bond of iniquity (Acts 8:23).

Looking diligently lest any man fail of the grace of God; lest any root of bitterness [Gk.: acridity, i.e., desire for revenge (carrying a grudge)] *springing up trouble you, and thereby many be defiled* (Hebrews 12:15).

ADULTERY—*Sin:* Idolatry; pornography. (See SEX.)

Ye [spiritual] *adulterers and adulteresses, know ye not that the friendship of the world is enmity with God?* (James 4:4a)

And I find more bitter than death the woman, whose heart is snares and nets, and her hands as bands: whoso pleaseth God shall escape from her; but the sinner shall be taken by her (Ecclesiastes 7:26).

Such is the way of an adulterous woman; she eateth, and wipeth her mouth, and saith, I have done no wickedness (Proverbs 30:20).

But I say unto you, That whosoever looketh on a woman to lust after her hath committed adultery with her already in his heart (Matthew 5:28).

ANKLES—*Faith:* **Weak Ankles** = *Weak faith;* unsupported; undependable.

And when the man that had the line in his hand went forth eastward, he measured a thousand cubits, and he brought me through the waters; the waters were to the ankles [faith, the first step into the Spirit (see KNEES, HIPS, and RIVER)] (Ezekiel 47:3).

ANTIQUES—*Past:* Inherited from our forefathers (good or evil); memories. (See ATTIC, *Section 2,* GRANDMOTHER, *Section 7,* and ROCKING CHAIR, *Section 9.*)

Thus saith the Lord, Stand ye in the ways, and see, and ask for the old paths, where is the good way, and walk therein, and ye shall find rest for your souls (Jeremiah 6:16a).

ANTLERS—See HORNS.

APPLES—*Fruit:* Words; sin; temptation; appreciation (as in "giving a teacher an apple"); fruit of the Spirit.

A word fitly spoken is like apples of gold [words of wisdom] *in pictures of silver* (Proverbs 25:11).

And when the woman saw that the tree was good for food, and that it was pleasant to the eyes, and a tree to be desired to make one wise, she took of the fruit thereof, and did eat, and gave also unto her husband with her; and he did eat (Genesis 3:6).

Either make the tree good, and his fruit good; or else make the tree corrupt, and his fruit corrupt: for the tree is known by his fruit. O generation of vipers, how can ye, being evil, speak good things? for out of the abundance of the heart the mouth speaketh (Matthew 12:33-34).

But the fruit of the Spirit is love, joy, peace, longsuffering, gentleness, goodness, faith, meekness, temperance: against such there is no law (Galatians 5:22-23).

ARM—*Strength or Weakness:* Savior; deliverer; helper; aid; reaching out (showing mercy); striker.

Who hath believed our report? and to whom is the arm of the Lord revealed? (Isaiah 53:1)

With a strong hand, and with a stretched out arm [reaching out to those in need]: *for His mercy endureth for ever* (Psalm 136:12).

For a bishop must be blameless, as the steward of God...not soon angry...no striker... (Titus 1:7).

Thus saith the Lord; Cursed be the man that trusteth in man, and maketh flesh his arm, and whose heart departeth from the Lord (Jeremiah 17:5).

ARROWS—See BOW/ARROWS.

ASHES—*Memories (that which has been reduced to ashes remains only in memory):* Repentance; ruin; destruction.

Your remembrances are like unto ashes... (Job 13:12).

Wherefore I abhor myself, and repent in dust and ashes [bringing sin to remembrance] (Job 42:6).

ATOM BOMB—*Power:* Holy Spirit outpouring (the atom bomb is both a sign of the last days and a parable of God's mighty power); miracle power; sudden destruction.

But ye shall receive power, after that the Holy Ghost is come upon you: and ye shall be witnesses unto Me both in Jerusalem, and in all Judea, and in Samaria, and unto the uttermost part of the earth (Acts 1:8).

And it shall come to pass in the last days, saith God, I will pour out of My Spirit upon all flesh.... And I will show wonders in heaven above, and signs in the earth beneath; blood, and fire, and vapor [pillar or column] *of smoke* [a description of the fireball and mushroom cloud of an atomic blast] (Acts 2:17,19).

For when they shall say, Peace and safety; then sudden destruction cometh upon them, as travail upon a woman with child; and they shall not escape (1 Thessalonians 5:3).

AUTUMN—*End:* Completion; change; repentance.

But we are all as an unclean thing, and all our righteousnesses are as filthy rags; and we all do fade as a leaf; and our iniquities, like the wind, have taken us away (Isaiah 64:6).

The harvest is past, the summer is ended, and we are not saved (Jeremiah 8:20).

AXE—*Word:* Gospel; preaching; exhorting others; rebuke; repentance.

And now also the axe [Word of God, i.e., command to repent] *is laid unto the root of the trees: therefore every tree which bringeth not forth good fruit is hewn down, and cast into the fire* (Matthew 3:10).

Iron sharpeneth iron; so a man sharpeneth the countenance of his friend [by exhorting or reproving him] (Proverbs 27:17).

If the iron [axe] *be blunt, and he do not whet the edge* [study God's Word to be able to use His wisdom and knowledge], *then must he put to more strength: but wisdom is profitable to direct* (Ecclesiastes 10:10).

BACK DOOR—See BACK, *Section 4*, and DOOR.

BASEBALL CARDS—*Hero Worship:* Esteem for another person (proper or improper).

And to esteem them very highly in love for their work's sake (1 Thessalonians 5:13a).

And there went out a champion out of the camp of the Philistines, named Goliath, of Gath, whose height was six cubits and a span (1 Samuel 17:4).

BASEBALL GAME—See PLAY.

BATHING—*Cleansing:* Sanctification; repentance; temptation. (See SOAP, WASHBASIN, and WASH-CLOTH.)

Wash me thoroughly from mine iniquity, and cleanse me from my sin. For I acknowledge my transgressions: and my sin is ever before me (Psalm 51:2-3).

Husbands, love your wives, even as Christ also loved the church, and gave Himself for it; that He might sanctify and cleanse it with the washing of water by the word (Ephesians 5:25-26).

And it came to pass in an eveningtide, that David arose from off his bed, and walked upon the roof of the king's house: and from the roof he saw a woman washing herself; and the woman was very beautiful to look upon (2 Samuel 11:2).

BEARD—*Covering:* Humanity; relating to the heart. **Rough, Unshaven Face** = *Spiritual neglect or uncleanness;* coarse or harsh personality. (See HAIR.)

> *They shall not make baldness upon their head, neither shall they shave off the corner of their beard...* [self-justification] (Leviticus 21:5).

BED—*Rest:* Salvation; meditation; intimacy; peace; covenant (as in marriage), or an evil covenant (as in natural or spiritual adultery); self-made (harmful) conditions (as in "You made your bed, now sleep in it!").

> *Stand in awe, and sin not: commune with your own heart upon your bed, and be still...* (Psalm 4:4).

> *If I ascend up into heaven, Thou art there: if I make my bed in hell, behold, Thou art there* [See Isaiah 28:18-20.] (Psalm 139:8).

> *Marriage is honorable in all, and the bed* [is to be kept] *undefiled: but whoremongers and adulterers God will judge* (Hebrews 13:4).

BELLS—*Sign indicating: 1. Change* (as in "the times are changing"). *2. God's Presence* (as in "the manifestation of the Spirit...the gift of tongues"). *3. Vanity* (when used as jewelry); pride.

> *A golden bell* [the gifts of the Spirit] *and a pomegranate* [the fruit of the Spirit], *a golden bell and a pomegranate, upon the hem of the robe* [of righteousness] *round about* (Exodus 28:34).

> *Though I speak with the tongues of men and of angels, and have not charity* [love], *I am become as...a tinkling cymbal* [or bell] (1 Corinthians 13:1).

Wherefore tongues [spiritual bells] *are for a sign, not to them that believe, but to them that believe not* (1 Corinthians 14:22a).

Moreover the Lord saith, Because the daughters of Zion are haughty, and walk with stretched forth necks and wanton eyes, walking and mincing as they go, and making a tinkling with [bells on] *their feet* (Isaiah 3:16).

BELLY—*Spirit:* Desire; lust; heart; feelings; selfishness; self-worship; sickness.

He that believeth on Me, as the scripture hath said, out of his belly [spirit] *shall flow rivers of living water* (John 7:38).

The words of a talebearer are as wounds, and they go down into the innermost parts of the belly [spirit or heart] (Proverbs 26:22).

Whose end is destruction, whose God is their belly [their own spirit, or self], *and whose glory is in their shame, who mind earthly things* (Philippians 3:19).

BESTIALITY—*Inordinate Lust:* Unnatural, deviant sex acts (as in oral or anal sex); obscene. (See SEX.)

Neither shalt thou lie [have sex] *with any beast to defile thyself therewith: neither shall any woman stand before a beast to lie down thereto: it is confusion* (Leviticus 18:23).

For this is the will of God, even your sanctification, that ye should abstain from fornication: that every one of you should know how to possess his vessel [wife] *in sanctification and honor; not in the lust of concupiscence* [strong, inordinate lust], *even as the Gentiles which know not God* (1 Thessalonians 4:3-5).

BIKINI—*Uncovered:* Carnal; seduction; temptation; insufficient covering.

Thy nakedness shall be uncovered, yea, thy shame shall be seen... (Isaiah 47:3).

BINGO—*Winner or Correct:* Sudden victory; correct answer, idea, or understanding.

Know ye not that they which run in a race [or compete in a game] *run all, but one receiveth the prize? So run, that ye may obtain* (1 Corinthians 9:24).

He saith unto them, But whom say ye that I am? And Simon Peter answered and said, Thou art the Christ, the Son of the living God (Matthew 16:15-16).

BINOCULARS—*Insight:* Understanding; prophetic vision; future event. **Not Focused (blurred)** = *Without understanding or insight.* (See TELESCOPE.)

Howbeit when He, the Spirit of truth, is come...He will show you things to come (John 16:13).

And not as Moses, which put a vail over his face, that the children of Israel could not stedfastly look to the end of that which is abolished (2 Corinthians 3:13).

BLADDER—See URINATING.

BLEEDING—*Wounded:* Hurt, naturally or emotionally; spiritually dying; offended; in strife; gossip; unclean. (See HOSPITAL, *Section 2*, and BLOOD, *Section 9*.)

He healeth the broken in heart, and bindeth up their wounds (Psalm 147:3).

The words of a talebearer are as wounds... (Proverbs 18:8).

BLIND—*Ignorance:* Unseeing; without understanding; foolish; self-justification and self-righteousness; hatred; sealed; unlearned.

Let them alone: they be blind leaders of the blind. And if the blind lead the blind, both shall fall into the ditch (Matthew 15:14).

Because thou sayest, I am rich, and increased with goods, and have need of nothing; and knowest not that thou art wretched, and miserable, and poor, and blind... [self-righteous, without understanding] (Revelation 3:17).

Thou blind [self-righteous] *Pharisee, cleanse first that which is within the cup and platter, that the outside of them may be clean also* (Matthew 23:26).

But he that lacketh these things is blind [self-righteous], *and cannot see afar off* [and is proud], *and hath forgotten that he was purged from his old sins* (2 Peter 1:9).

But he that hateth his brother is in darkness, and walketh in darkness, and knoweth not whither he goeth, because that darkness hath blinded his eyes (1 John 2:11).

BLOOD—*Life of the Flesh:* Covenant; murder; defiled; unclean; pollution; purging; testimony; witness; guilt.

For the life of the flesh is in the blood (Leviticus 17:11a).

Cursed be he that taketh reward to slay an innocent person [such as a doctor in performing an abortion for pay]... (Deuteronomy 27:25).

And shed innocent blood, even the blood of their sons and of their daughters [through abortion], *whom they sacrificed unto the idols of Canaan* [or convenience]: *and the land was polluted with blood* (Psalm 106:38).

And if a woman have an issue, and her issue in her flesh be blood, she shall be put apart seven days: and whosoever toucheth her shall be unclean until the even (Leviticus 15:19).

When I say unto the wicked, O wicked man, thou shalt surely die; if thou dost not speak to warn the wicked from his way, that wicked man shall die in his iniquity; but his blood will I require at thine hand (Ezekiel 33:8).

BLOOD TRANSFUSION—*Change:* Regeneration; salvation; deliverance.

Not by works of righteousness which we have done, but according to His mercy He saved us, by the washing of regeneration, and renewing of the Holy Ghost (Titus 3:5).

And be not conformed to this world: but be ye transformed by the renewing of your mind, that ye may prove what is that good, and acceptable, and perfect, will of God (Romans 12:2).

BODY ODOR—*Uncleanness:* Bad attitude; filthiness of the flesh; rejected.

Having therefore these promises, dearly beloved, let us cleanse ourselves from all filthiness of the flesh and spirit, perfecting holiness in the fear of God [See James 4:8.] (2 Corinthians 7:1).

Wherefore lay apart all filthiness and superfluity of naughtiness (James 1:21a).

Dead flies cause the ointment of the apothecary to send forth a stinking savor: so doth a little folly him that is in reputation for wisdom and honor (Ecclesiastes 10:1).

BOLTS—See NUTS AND BOLTS.

BONES—*Spirit:* Condition of the heart; death; that which is eternal.

Woe unto you, scribes and Pharisees, hypocrites! for ye are like unto whited sepulchres, which indeed appear beautiful outward, but are within full of dead men's bones, and of all uncleanness (Matthew 23:27).

Then He said unto me, Son of man, these bones are the whole house of Israel: behold, they say, Our bones are dried, and our hope is lost: we are cut off for our parts (Ezekiel 37:11).

A merry heart doeth good like a medicine: but a broken spirit drieth the bones (Proverbs 17:22).

BOOK—*Record:* Word of God; heart of man; witness; remembrance (good or evil); conscience; education; knowledge. (See LIBRARY, *Section 2.*)

And I saw the dead, small and great, stand before God; and the books were opened: and another book was opened, which is the book of life: and the dead were judged out of those things which were written in the books [their hearts], according to their works (Revelation 20:12).

Then they that feared the Lord spake often one to another: and the Lord hearkened, and heard it, and a book of remembrance was written before Him for them that feared the Lord, and that thought upon His name (Malachi 3:16).

Ye are our epistle written in our hearts, known and read of all men (2 Corinthians 3:2).

BOOTS—See SHOES/BOOTS.

BOW/ARROWS—*Words or Person:* Accusations; slander; gossip; prayer; deliverance. **Bow** = *Tongue;* Power. **Quiver** = *Heart.* **Arrows** = *Words.*

Who whet their tongue like a sword, and bend their bows to shoot their arrows, even bitter words (Psalm 64:3).

For, lo, the wicked bend their bow, they make ready their arrow upon the string, that they may privily [secretly] *shoot at the upright in heart* (Psalm 11:2).

A man that beareth false witness against his neighbor is a maul, and a sword, and a sharp arrow (Proverbs 25:18).

And he said, Open the window eastward. And he opened it. Then Elisha said, Shoot. And he shot. And he said, The arrow of the Lord's deliverance...for thou shalt smite the Syrians...till thou have consumed them (2 Kings 13:17).

And He [God] *hath made my mouth like a sharp sword; in the shadow of His hand hath He hid me, and made me a polished* [arrow] *shaft; in His quiver* [heart] *hath He hid me* (Isaiah 49:2).

BOWL—See POT/PAN/BOWL.

BOXING—*Striving:* Preaching; deliverance; trial; tribulation. (See WRESTLING.)

I have fought a good fight, I have finished my course, I have kept the faith (2 Timothy 4:7).

And every man that striveth for the mastery is temperate in all things. Now they do it to obtain a corruptible crown; but we an incorruptible. I therefore so run, not as uncertainly; so fight I, not as one that beateth the air [shadow boxing] (1 Corinthians 9:25-26).

BREAD—*Life or Word:* Doctrine; covenant; the Church; substance; provision (money, food, etc.).

But He answered and said, It is written, Man shall not live by bread alone, but by every word that proceedeth out of the mouth of God (Matthew 4:4).

And when Gideon was come, behold, there was a man that told a dream unto his fellow, and said, Behold, I dreamed a dream, and, lo, a cake of barley bread [common man's bread] *tumbled into the host of Midian, and came unto a tent, and smote it that it fell, and overturned it, that the tent lay along. And his fellow answered and said, This* [bread] *is nothing else save the sword* [Word of God in the hand] *of Gideon the Son of Joash, a man of Israel: for into his hand hath God delivered Midian, and all the host* (Judges 7:13-14).

I speak not of you all: I know whom I have chosen: but that the scripture may be fulfilled, He that eateth bread [made a covenant] *with Me hath lifted up his heel* [betrayal] *against Me* [See EATING.] (John 13:18).

Neither did we eat any man's bread for nought; but wrought with labor and travail night and day, that we might not be chargeable to any of you (2 Thessalonians 3:8).

BREAD, MOLDY—*Unfit:* Tradition; without revelation; stale; defiled.

And all the bread of their provision was dry and mouldy [man under the law] (Joshua 9:5b).

Ye offer polluted [molded] *bread upon Mine altar; and ye say, Wherein have we polluted Thee? In that ye say, The table of the Lord is contemptible* (Malachi 1:7).

Therefore let us keep the feast, not with old leaven, neither with the leaven of malice and wickedness; but with the un-leavened [or unmolded] *bread of sincerity and truth* (1 Corinthians 5:8).

Why do Thy disciples transgress the tradition of the elders? for they wash not their hands when they eat bread. But He answered and said unto them, Why do ye also transgress the commandment of God by your tradition? ...Thus have ye made the commandment [bread] *of God of none effect* [useless, as molded bread] *by your tradition* (Matthew 15:2-3,6).

BRIDGE—*Support or Way:* Faith; trial (of faith); joined.

And he rose up that night, and took his two wives, and his two womenservants, and his eleven sons, and passed over the ford [Heb.: "a crossing place"] *Jabbok* (Genesis 32:22).

When thou passest through the waters, I will be with thee; and through the rivers, they shall not overflow thee (Isaiah 43:2a).

There hath no temptation [trial] *taken you but such as is common to man: but God is faithful, who will not suffer you to be tempted above that ye are able; but will with the temptation also make a way* [bridge] *to escape, that ye may be able to bear it* (1 Corinthians 10:13).

BRIERS—*Snare:* Obstacle; hindrance; trial; wicked person; rejected; cursed. (For stickers or burrs, see THORNS.)

Upon the land of my people shall come up thorns and briers (Isaiah 32:13a).

The best of them is as a brier: the most upright is sharper than a thorn hedge (Micah 7:4a).

But that which beareth thorns and briers is rejected, and is nigh unto cursing; whose end is to be burned (Hebrews 6:8).

BROOM—*Cleaning or Witchcraft:* Clean house (put away sin). (See SWEEPING.)

And when He had made a scourge of small cords, He drove them all out of the temple, and the sheep, and the oxen; and poured out the changers' money, and overthrew the tables (John 2:15).

Thou shalt not suffer a witch to live (Exodus 22:18).

Now the works of the flesh are manifest, which are these...witchcraft [manipulation and control] (Galatians 5:19-20a).

BUBBLE GUM—*Childish:* Foolishness; immaturity.

The heart of him that hath understanding seeketh knowledge: but the mouth of fools feedeth on foolishness (Proverbs 15:14).

Foolishness is bound in the heart of a child; but the rod of correction shall drive it far from him (Proverbs 22:15).

BULLETS—See GUNS/BULLETS.

BUTTER—*Works:* Doing (or not doing) the Word or will of God. (See CHEESE for explanation); deceptive motives, words, or works; smooth talker; deceiver.

The words of his mouth were smoother than butter, but war was in his heart: his words were softer than oil, yet were they drawn swords (Psalm 55:21).

Surely the churning of milk bringeth forth butter...so the forcing of wrath bringeth forth strife (Proverbs 30:33).

Butter [knowledge gained through experience (see Heb. 5:12-14)] *and honey* [Holy Spirit] *shall he eat, that he may know to refuse the evil, and choose the good* (Isaiah 7:15).

CALENDAR—*Time:* Date; event; appointment. (See CLOCK, *Section 9*, for specific numbers see *Section 6*.)

Also, O Judah, he hath set [a date for] *an harvest* [of retribution] *for thee, when I returned the captivity of My people* (Hosea 6:11).

CARDS—*Facts:* Honesty (as in "putting all your cards on the table"); truth; expose or reveal; dishonesty; underhanded dealing; cheating; wisdom (as in "knowing when to hold and when to fold").

Provide things honest in the sight of all men (Romans 12:17b).

CARNIVAL—*Worldly:* Festivity; party spirit; exhibitionism; divination; competition. (See ROLLER COASTER, *Section 8*.)

And take heed to yourselves, lest at any time your hearts be overcharged with surfeiting, and drunkenness, and cares of this life, and so that day come upon you unawares (Luke 21:34).

And it came to pass, as we went to prayer, a certain damsel possessed with a spirit of divination met us, which brought her masters much gain by soothsaying [fortune-telling] (Acts 16:16).

CHAIR—*Rest or Position:* Quietness; position of authority (as in "chair of a board meeting").

For thus saith the Lord God, the Holy One of Israel; In returning and rest shall ye be saved; in quietness and in confidence shall be your strength... (Isaiah 30:15).

And love the uppermost rooms at feasts, and the chief seats in the synagogues (Matthew 23:6).

CHECK (Bank)—*Faith (the currency of the Kingdom of God):* Provision; trust. **Bad Check** = *Fraud;* deception; hypocrisy; lack of faith or prayer.

Now faith is the substance of things hoped for, the evidence of things not seen (Hebrews 11:1).

And He said unto them, Why are ye so fearful? how is it that ye have no faith [as in an overdrawn account]? (Mark 4:40)

And the apostles said unto the Lord, Increase our faith (Luke 17:5).

CHEESE—*Works:* Doing (or not doing) the Word or will of God. (See BUTTER.)

Jesus saith unto them, My meat [solid food] *is to do the will of Him that sent Me, and to finish His work* [i.e., butter and cheese is liquid milk (God's Word) made into solid food (God's work). Compare First Peter 2:2: "As newborn babes, desire the sincere milk of the word, that ye may grow thereby (become mature doers of the Word)."] (John 4:34).

Hast Thou not poured me out as milk, and curdled me like cheese? (Job 10:10)

CHEWING—*Meditate (as in, "let me chew on that awhile"):* Receiving wisdom and understanding. **Chewing Bubble Gum** = *Childishness;* foolishness. **Chewing Tough Meat** = *Hard saying or difficult work.* (See EATING, FOOD/MILK, and TEETH.)

> *Meditate [chew] upon these things; give thyself wholly to them; that thy profiting may appear to all* (1 Timothy 4:15).

> *My mouth shall speak of wisdom; and the meditation of my heart shall be of understanding* (Psalm 49:3).

> *The thought [meditation, or planning] of foolishness is sin: and the scorner is an abomination to men* (Proverbs 24:9).

CHOKING—*Hindrance:* Stumbling over something (as in "too much to swallow"); hatred or anger (as in "I could choke him!"); unfruitful (as in "the weeds choked the tomatoes").

> *And the cares of this world, and the deceitfulness of riches, and the lusts of other things entering in, choke the word, and it becometh unfruitful* (Mark 4:19).

CHRISTMAS—*Gift:* Season of rejoicing; spiritual gifts; a surprise; good will; benevolence; commercialism.

> *If ye then, being evil, know how to give good gifts unto your children: how much more shall your heavenly Father give the Holy Spirit to them that ask Him?* (Luke 11:13)

> *Follow after charity, and desire spiritual gifts, but rather that ye may prophesy* (1 Corinthians 14:1).

CHURCH SERVICE—*Worship:* True or false worship; tradition.

God is a Spirit: and they that worship Him must worship Him in spirit and in truth (John 4:24).

Howbeit in vain do they worship Me, teaching for doctrines the commandments of men (Mark 7:7).

CIGARETTES—See SMOKING.

CIVIL TRIAL—See COURTHOUSE, *Section 2.*

CLOCK—*Time:* Late; early; delay. **Grandfather Clock** = *Past* (for significant numbers see *Section 6*). (See CALENDAR.)

Redeeming the time, because the days are evil (Ephesians 5:16).

CLOSET—*Private:* Personal; prayer; secret sin (as in "skeletons in the closet"); something hidden.

But thou, when thou prayest, enter into thy closet, and when thou hast shut thy door, pray to thy Father which is in secret; and thy Father which seeth in secret shall reward thee openly (Matthew 6:6).

For nothing [good or evil] *is secret, that shall not be made manifest; neither any thing hid, that shall not be known and come abroad* (Luke 8:17).

For there is nothing covered, that shall not be revealed; neither hid, that shall not be known (Luke 12:2).

CLOTHING—*Covering:* Righteousness; spirit (attitude). **Filthy Clothes** = *Unrighteousness;* self-righteousness; uncleanness. (See COAT and SKIRT.)

But put ye on the Lord Jesus Christ, and make not provision for the flesh, to fulfil the lusts thereof (Romans 13:14).

Let thy priests be clothed with righteousness (Psalm 132:9a).

For if there come unto your assembly a man with a gold ring [self-glorification], *in goodly apparel, and there come in also a poor man in vile raiment* (James 2:2).

But we are all as an unclean thing, and all our righteousnesses are as filthy rags (Isaiah 64:6a).

As he clothed himself with cursing like as with his garment, so let it come into his bowels like water, and like oil into his bones (Psalm 109:18).

CLOUDS—*Change or Covering:* Trouble; distress; threatening; thoughts (of trouble); confusion; hidden; covered (see FOG). **White Clouds** = *Good change;* glory; revival.

That day is a day of wrath, a day of trouble and distress, a day of wasteness and desolation, a day of darkness and gloominess, a day of clouds and thick darkness (Zephaniah 1:15).

Ask ye of the Lord rain in the time of the latter rain; so the Lord shall make bright clouds, and give them showers of rain [revival], *to every one grass in the field* (Zechariah 10:1).

COAT—*Covering:* Anointing; authority; protection; grief; shame; confusion. **Shirt** = *Covering as pertaining to the heart: i.e., righteousness or sin.* **Without a Shirt (male or female)** = *Self-righteousness (self-justification);* legalism; shame, temptation. (See CLOTHING.)

And he took the mantle of Elijah that fell from him, and smote the waters, and said, Where is the Lord God of Elijah? and when he also had smitten the waters, they parted hither and thither: and Elisha went over. And when the sons of the prophets which were to view at Jericho saw him, they said, The spirit [anointing, and therefore the authority] *of Elijah doth rest on Elisha* (2 Kings 2:14-15a).

As he loved cursing, so let it come unto him: as he delighted not in blessing, so let it be far from him. As he clothed himself with cursing like as with his garment, so let it come into his bowels like water, and like oil into his bones. Let it be unto him as the garment which covereth him, and for a girdle wherewith he is girded continually (Psalm 109:17-19).

Let mine adversaries be clothed with shame, and let them cover themselves with their own confusion, as with a mantle (Psalm 109:29).

COFFEE—*Bitter or Stimulant:* Desire for revenge (bitter envying); bitter memories; wake-up call; become sober.

But if ye have bitter envying and strife in your hearts, glory not, and lie not against the truth (James 3:14).

Wherefore he saith, Awake thou that sleepest, and arise from the dead, and Christ shall give thee light (Ephesians 5:14).

Young men likewise exhort to be sober minded (Titus 2:6).

COMPASS—See MAP.

CORD—See ROPE/CORD.

CORNET—See TRUMPET.

CORNUCOPIA (Horn of Plenty)—*Abundance:* Abundance without measure or limitation; goodness without end; blessed.

And all these blessings shall come on thee, and overtake thee, if thou shalt hearken unto the voice of the Lord thy God. ... Blessed shall be the fruit of thy body, and the fruit of thy ground, and the fruit of thy cattle, the increase of thy kine, and the flocks of thy sheep. Blessed shall be thy basket and thy store (Deuteronomy 28:2,4-5).

But the fruit of the Spirit is love, joy, peace, longsuffering, gentleness, goodness, faith, meekness, temperance: against such there is no law (Galatians 5:22-23).

Now unto him that is able to do exceeding abundantly above all that we ask or think, according to the power that worketh in us (Ephesians 3:20).

COUCH—*Rest:* At ease; unconcerned; lazy (as in "couch potato").

His soul shall dwell at ease; and his seed shall inherit the earth (Psalm 25:13).

That lie upon beds of ivory, and stretch themselves upon their couches, and eat the lambs out of the flock, and the calves out of the midst of the stall (Amos 6:4).

CROSSROADS—*Decision:* Confusion; choice; job change; career change; geographical move. **Right Turn** = *Natural change.* **Left Turn** = *Spiritual change.* (See RIGHT and LEFT, *Section 4.*)

And a certain ruler asked Him, saying, Good Master, what shall I do to inherit eternal life? ... Now when Jesus heard these things, He said unto him, Yet lackest thou one thing: sell all that thou hast, and distribute unto the poor, and thou shalt have treasure in heaven: and come, follow Me [forsaking both riches and positions of authority].

And when he heard this [requirement to change, both naturally and spiritually], *he was very sorrowful: for he was very rich* (Luke 18:18,22-23).

CROWN—*Authority or Reward:* Rule; honor; glory; power; promotion.

And he brought forth the king's son, and put the crown upon him...and they made him king, and anointed him...and said, God save the king (2 Kings 11:12).

And when the chief Shepherd shall appear, ye shall receive a crown of glory [reward] *that fadeth not away* (1 Peter 5:4).

CRYING (as in **weeping**)— See TEARS.

CRYING OUT—See TELEPHONE.

CRYSTAL BALL—*Vision:* Future; divination; fortune telling; prediction.

Then the Lord said unto me, The prophets prophesy lies in My name: I sent them not, neither have I commanded them, neither spake unto them: they prophesy unto you a false vision and divination, and a thing of nought, and the deceit of their heart (Jeremiah 14:14).

And it came to pass, as we went to prayer, a certain damsel possessed with a spirit of divination met us, which brought her masters much gain by soothsaying [fortune telling] (Acts 16:16).

CURTAIN—See VAIL.

DAM—*Power:* Potential; reserve; source of (or potential for) great power; block; restriction; hindrance; a way over an obstacle (as a hunter crossing a stream on a beaver dam). (See BEAVER, *Section 1*, BRIDGE and WATER, *Section 9*.)

> *That the waters which came down from above stood and rose up upon an heap* [were temporarily restricted or stopped from flowing] *very far from the city Adam...and those* [waters] *that came down toward the sea of the plain, even the salt sea, failed, and were cut off: and the people passed over right against Jericho* (Joshua 3:16).

DANCING—*Worship:* Idolatry; prophesying (true or false); joy; romance; seduction; lewdness. (See PLAY.)

> *And it came to pass, as soon as he came nigh unto the camp, that he saw the* [golden] *calf, and the dancing* [idol worship]*: and Moses' anger waxed hot, and he cast the tables out of his hands, and brake them beneath the mount* [See First Corinthians 10:7.] (Exodus 32:19).

> *Let them praise His name in the dance* (Psalm 149:3a).

> *The joy of our heart is ceased; our dance is turned into mourning* (Lamentations 5:15).

> *But when Herod's birthday was kept, the daughter of Herodias* [belly] *danced before them, and pleased* [lustful] *Herod* (Matthew 14:6).

DARKNESS—See NIGHT.

DAY—*Light:* Knowledge; truth; manifest; good; evil revealed. (See LIGHT.)

> *And God saw the light, that it was good: and God divided the light from the darkness. And God called the light Day, and the darkness he called Night* (Genesis 1:4-5a).

> *Every man's work shall be made manifest: for the day shall declare it...* (1 Corinthians 3:13).

But all things that are reproved are made manifest by the light [of day]: *for whatsoever doth make manifest is light* (Ephesians 5:13).

DEATH—*Termination:* Repentance; loss; sorrow; failure; separation; the end of a relationship; physical death, when naturally interpreted.

Verily, verily, I say unto you, Except a corn of wheat fall into the ground and die, it abideth alone: but if it die, it bringeth forth much fruit (John 12:24).

I protest by your rejoicing which I have in Christ Jesus our Lord, I die daily (1 Corinthians 15:31).

Forasmuch then as the children are partakers of flesh and blood, He also Himself likewise took part of the same; that through death He might destroy him that had the power of death, that is, the devil (Hebrews 2:14).

They are dead, they shall not live; they are deceased, they shall not rise: therefore hast Thou visited and destroyed them, and made all their memory to perish (Isaiah 26:14).

DEED—See TITLE/DEED.

DEER HUNTING—See DEER, *Section 1*.

DESERT—*Barren:* Unproductive; dry; spiritual wasteland; without hope.

They wandered in the wilderness in a solitary way; they found no city to dwell in. Hungry and thirsty, their soul fainted in them (Psalm 107:4-5).

DIAMOND—*Hard:* Unchangeable; hardheaded; hardhearted; eternal (as in "a diamond is forever"). Gift of the Spirit; something valuable or precious.

Behold, I have made thy face strong against their faces, and thy forehead strong against their foreheads. As an adamant [diamond], harder than flint have I made thy forehead (Ezekiel 3:8-9a).

Yea, they made their hearts as an adamant stone [diamond], lest they should hear the law, and the words which the Lord of hosts hath sent in His spirit by the former prophets: therefore came a great wrath from the Lord of hosts (Zechariah 7:12).

A gift is as a precious stone in the eyes of him that hath it: whithersoever it turneth, it prospereth (Proverbs 17:8).

DISH—See POT/PAN/BOWL.

DITCH—*Habit or Snare:* Religious tradition; addiction; lust; passion; sin.

Let them [religious leaders] alone: they be blind leaders of the blind. And if the blind lead the blind, both shall fall into the ditch (Matthew 15:14).

He made a pit, and digged it, and is fallen into the ditch which he made (Psalm 7:15).

For a whore is a deep ditch; and a strange woman is a narrow pit (Proverbs 23:27).

DOMINOES—*Continuous:* Chain reaction (as with dominos, each causing the next one to fall).

And they shall fall one upon another... (Leviticus 26:37).

DOOR—*Entrance:* Christ; (new) opportunity; way; avenue; mouth.

Then said Jesus unto them again, Verily, verily, I say unto you, I am the door of the sheep (John 10:7).

Withal praying also for us, that God would open unto us a door of utterance, to speak the mystery of Christ... (Colossians 4:3).

Set a watch, O Lord, before my mouth; keep the door of my lips (Psalm 141:3).

DREAMING (dreaming that you are dreaming)— *Message:* A message within a message; aspiration; vision. (See SLEEP.)

And they said unto him, We have dreamed a dream, and there is no interpreter of it. And Joseph said unto them, Do not interpretations belong to God? (Genesis 40:8a)

DRESS—See COAT.

DRINKING FOUNTAIN—See WATER FOUNTAIN.

DROUGHT—See RAIN.

DROWNING—*Overcome:* Self-pity; depression; grief; sorrow; temptation; backslid; excessive debt. (See FLOOD.)

But they that will be rich fall into temptation and a snare, and into many foolish and hurtful lusts, which drown men in destruction and perdition (1 Timothy 6:9).

To appoint unto them that mourn in Zion, to give unto them beauty for ashes, the oil [anointing] *of joy for mourning, the garment of praise for* [those who are drowning in] *the spirit of heaviness...* (Isaiah 61:3).

DRUGS—*Influence:* Spell; sorcery; witchcraft; control; religion (legalism); medicine; healing. (See WITCH, *Section 7.*)

For rebellion is as the sin of witchcraft... (1 Samuel 15:23).

O foolish Galatians, who hath bewitched you, that ye should not obey the truth? (Galatians 3:1a)

A merry heart doeth good like a medicine... (Proverbs 17:22).

DYNAMITE—*Power:* Miracle; potential; danger; destruction.

But when the multitudes saw it [the miracle of healing], *they marvelled, and glorified God, which had given such power unto men* (Matthew 9:8).

Behold, I give unto you power to tread on serpents and scorpions, and over all the power of the enemy... (Luke 10:19).

When I was daily with you in the temple, ye stretched forth no hands against Me: but this is your hour, and the power of darkness (Luke 22:53).

EARTHQUAKE—*Upheaval:* Change (by crisis), thus repentance; trial; God's judgment; disaster; trauma; shock.

And suddenly there was a great earthquake, so that the foundations of the prison were shaken (Acts 16:26a).

Thou shalt be [judged and therefore] *visited of the Lord of hosts with thunder, and with earthquake, and great noise, with storm and tempest, and the flame of devouring fire* (Isaiah 29:6).

Whose voice then shook the earth: but now He hath promised, saying, Yet once more I shake not the earth only, but also heaven. And this word, Yet once more, signifieth the removing of those things that are shaken, as of things that are made, that those things which cannot be shaken may remain (Hebrews 12:26-27).

EATING—*Partake:* Participate; experience; out-working; covenant; agreement; friendship; fellowship; devour; consume. (See CHEWING, FOOD/MILK, and TEETH.)

Jesus saith unto them, My meat is to do the will of Him that sent Me, and to finish His work (John 4:34).

Such is the way of an adulterous woman; she eateth, and wipeth her mouth, and saith, I have done no wickedness (Proverbs 30:20).

And I took the little book out of the angel's hand, and ate it up; and it [God's promises] *was in my mouth sweet as honey: and as soon as I had eaten* [experienced] *it, my belly was bitter* [working out our salvation is always with tribulation (see Acts 14:22; Phil. 2:12)] (Revelation 10:10).

And the men took of their victuals [ate with them], *and asked not counsel at the mouth of the Lord. And Joshua...made a league* [covenant] *with them, to let them live...* (Joshua 9:14-15).

...He that eateth bread [declaring his friendship, or agreement] *with Me hath lifted up his heel against Me* (John 13:18).

ECHO—*Repetition:* Gossip; accusation; voice of many; mocking; mimic.

But they cried, saying, Crucify Him, crucify Him (Luke 23:21).

EGG—*Promise:* Promising new thought; plan; potential; revelation; fragile. **Rotten Egg** = *Bad Person* (as in "he's a bad egg"); a person who breaks promises; bad company; bad idea; uncertainty (as in "don't count your eggs before they hatch"); without promise.

Or if he shall ask an egg [that which has been promised], *will he offer him a scorpion?* (Luke 11:12)

Meditate upon these things [brood over them]; *give thyself wholly to them* [hatch them out and feed the hatchlings]; *that thy profiting may appear to all* (1 Timothy 4:15).

ELECTRICITY—*Power:* Holy Spirit or sorcery. **Power Lines** = *Spiritual power;* dangerous obstacle when flying (see AIRPLANE). **Electrical Outlet** = *Power source;* Holy Spirit. **Burned Power Outlet** = *Offense;* anger. **Power Cord Unplugged** = *No power;* lack of prayer; lack of authority. (See LIGHTNING.)

For the kingdom of God is not in word, but in power (1 Corinthians 4:20).

But ye shall receive power, after that the Holy Ghost is come upon you... (Acts 1:8).

Even him, whose coming is after the working of Satan with all power and signs and lying wonders (2 Thessalonians 2:9).

ELEVATOR—*Changing Position:* Going into the spiritual ream; elevated. **Going Down** = *Demotion or trial;* backsliding. (For significant floor numbers, see *Section 6.*)

After this I looked, and, behold, a door was opened in heaven: and the first voice which I heard...said, Come up hither, and I will show thee things which must be hereafter (Revelation 4:1).

The wise shall inherit glory: but shame shall be the promotion of fools (Proverbs 3:35).

EXPLOSION—*Sudden:* Sudden expansion or increase (as in "that church has had explosive growth since the new pastor arrived"); swift change; destruction. (See VOLCANO.)

I have declared the former things from the beginning; and they went forth out of My mouth, and I showed them; I did them suddenly, and they came to pass (Isaiah 48:3).

EYES—*Desire (Good or Evil):* Covetousness; passion; lust; revelation; understanding; the window to the soul (thus revealing what is in the heart). **Winking** = *Deceitfulness or cunning;* hiding true desire. **Eyes Tightly Closed** = *Unbelief;* willful ignorance.

The light of the body is the eye: therefore when thine eye is single, thy whole body also is full of light; but when thine eye is evil, thy body also is full of darkness (Luke 11:34).

Wilt thou set thine eyes [desire] *upon that which is not? for riches certainly make themselves wings; they fly away as an eagle toward heaven* (Proverbs 23:5).

Hell and destruction are never full; so the eyes [passions] *of man are never satisfied* (Proverbs 27:20).

I will set no wicked thing before mine eyes... (Psalm 101:3).

The eyes of your understanding being enlightened... (Ephesians 1:18).

He [the deceitful man] *winketh with his eyes, he speaketh with his feet, he teacheth with his fingers* (Proverbs 6:13).

And the times of this ignorance [idolatry] *God winked at; but now commandeth all men every where to repent* (Acts 17:30).

They have not known nor understood: for He hath shut their eyes, that they cannot see; and their hearts, that they cannot understand (Isaiah 44:18).

FACE—*Heart:* Sad; glad; mad; bad; etc.; the same as another person (when one looks into the mirror of another person's heart, he see his own heart's reflection (see Prov. 27:19 below); before or against another person (as in "get out of my face!"); the actual person's face.

As in water face answereth to face, so the heart of man to [the heart of] *man* [See Romans 2:1.] (Proverbs 27:19).

He was a mighty hunter before [Heb.: "in the face of," i.e., against] *the Lord: wherefore it is said, Even as Nimrod the mighty hunter before the Lord* (Genesis 10:9).

FAIR—See CARNIVAL.

FALL—See AUTUMN.

FALLING—*Unsupported:* Loss of support (financial, moral, public, etc.); trial; succumb; backsliding.

He that trusteth in his riches shall fall: but the righteous shall flourish as a branch (Proverbs 11:28).

My brethren, count it all joy when ye fall into divers temptations (James 1:2).

Pride goeth before destruction, and an haughty spirit before a fall (Proverbs 16:18).

The mouth of strange women is a deep pit: he that is ab-horred of the Lord shall fall therein (Proverbs 22:14).

FEATHERS—*Covering:* Spirit. **Wet Feathers** = *Offense* (as in "madder than a wet hen"); weightless. (See WINGS.)

He shall cover thee with His feathers, and under His wings shalt thou trust: His truth shall be thy shield and buckler (Psalm 91:4).

FEET—*Heart:* Walk; way; thoughts (meditation); offense; stubborn (when unmovable); rebellion (when kicking); sin. **Lame Feet** = *Unbelief or error;* doubt. **Diseased Feet** = *Offense* (toward God or man). **Barefoot** = *Without preparation;* without understanding; without protection; without salvation; novice (as in "tenderfoot"); easily offended (as in tender feet). (See SHOES, SOCKS, and ANKLE.)

And your feet [heart] *shod with the preparation of the gospel of peace* (Ephesians 6:15).

And make straight paths for your feet, lest that which is lame be turned out of the way; but let it rather be healed. ... Looking diligently lest any man fail of the grace of God; lest any root of bitterness springing up trouble you, and thereby many be defiled (Hebrews 12:13,15).

[Unwise] *Confidence in an unfaithful man in time of trouble is like a...foot out of joint* [unfaithful, cannot be trusted, it will not support your weight] (Proverbs 25:19).

And he said, Who art Thou, Lord? And the Lord said, I am Jesus whom thou [hast rebelled against and therefore] *persecutest: it is hard for thee to kick against the pricks* (Acts 9:5).

Then Asa was wroth with the seer, and put him in a prison house; for he was in a rage with him because of this thing. And Asa oppressed some of the people the same time. ... And Asa...was diseased in his feet, until his disease was exceeding great: yet in his disease he sought not to the Lord, but to the physicians [his heart was wrong but he would not repent] (2 Chronicles 16:10,12).

FENCE—*Boundaries:* Barrier; obstacles; religious traditions; doctrines; inhibitions.

And the Lord said, Behold, the people is one, and they have all one language; and this they begin to do: and now nothing will be restrained [Heb.: "fenced"] *from them, which they have imagined to do* (Genesis 11:6).

And I will make thee unto this people a fenced brasen wall: and they shall fight against thee, but they shall not prevail against thee: for I am with thee to save thee and to deliver thee, saith the Lord (Jeremiah 15:20).

FIELD—*World:* God's work; harvest; opportunity; mixed multitude.

The field is the world; the good seed are the children of the kingdom; but the tares are the children of the wicked one (Matthew 13:38).

Say not ye, There are yet four months, and then cometh harvest? behold, I say unto you, Lift up your eyes, and look on the fields; for they are white already to harvest (John 4:35).

For Demas hath forsaken me, having loved this present world (2 Timothy 4:10a).

FINDING ITEMS—See LOST and FOUND.

FINGER—*Feeling:* Sensitivity; discernment; conviction; works. **Pointing Finger** = *Accusation;* direction (as in "he went that way"); instruction.

And He gave unto Moses, when He had made an end of communing with him upon mount Sinai, two tables of testimony, tables of stone, written with the finger [Spirit] *of God* (Exodus 31:18).

But if I with the finger [conviction of the Spirit] *of God cast out devils, no doubt the kingdom of God is come upon you* [see LICE] (Luke 11:20).

Then shalt thou call, and the Lord shall answer; thou shalt cry, and He shall say, Here I am. If thou take away from the midst of thee the yoke, the putting forth of the finger [pointing an accusing finger at others], *and speaking vanity* (Isaiah 58:9).

Their land also is full of idols; they worship the work of their own hands, that which their own fingers have made (Isaiah 2:8).

He winketh with his eyes, he speaketh with his feet, he teacheth with his fingers [works, or the example of his own life] (Proverbs 6:13).

FIRE/HEAT—*Passion:* Power; God's Word or Spirit; revival; anger; envy; jealousy; strife; desire; lust; zeal; trial; affliction; gossip. **Fireplace** = *Heart.* (See OVEN.)

Is not My word like as a fire? saith the Lord; and like a hammer that breaketh the rock [stony heart] *in pieces?* (Jeremiah 23:29)

Wherefore thus saith the Lord God of hosts, Because ye speak this word, behold, I will make My words in thy mouth fire, and this people wood, and it shall devour them (Jeremiah 5:14).

I indeed baptize you with water unto repentance: but He that cometh after me is mightier than I, whose shoes I am not worthy to bear: He shall baptize you with the Holy Ghost, and with fire [power and purification] (Matthew 3:11).

Even so the tongue is a little member, and boasteth great things. Behold, how great a matter a little fire kindleth! And the tongue is a fire, a world of iniquity: so is the tongue among our members, that it defileth the whole body, and setteth on fire the course of nature; and it is set on fire of hell (James 3:5-6).

But if they cannot contain, let them marry: for it is better to marry than to burn (1 Corinthians 7:9).

How long, Lord? wilt Thou be angry for ever? shall Thy jealousy burn like fire? (Psalm 79:5)

How long, Lord? wilt Thou hide thyself for ever? shall Thy wrath burn like fire? (Psalm 89:46)

Where no wood is, there the fire goeth out: so where there is no talebearer, the strife ceaseth (Proverbs 26:20).

If fire [gossip or slander] *break out, and catch in thorns* [becomes a hindrance or curse to one's neighbor], *so that the stacks of corn, or the standing corn, or the field, be consumed therewith; he that kindled the fire* [started the gossip or slander] *shall surely make restitution* (Exodus 22:6).

FIREWOOD—See WOOD.

FISHING—*Hope:* Witnessing; evangelizing; preaching; discouragement (without hope).

And He saith unto them, Follow Me, and I will make you fishers of men (Matthew 4:19).

Or saith He it altogether for our sakes? For our sakes, no doubt, this is written: that he that ploweth [or fishes (preaches)] *should plow in hope; and that he that thresheth in hope should be partaker of his hope* (1 Corinthians 9:10).

Simon Peter saith unto them, I go a fishing. They say unto him, We also go with thee. They went forth, and entered into a ship immediately; and that night they caught nothing [discouraged, hopelessness] (John 21:3).

FLASHLIGHT—See LIGHT.

FLOOD—*Overwhelm:* Temptation; sin; judgment; depression; overcome. (See DROWN.)

...When the enemy shall come in like a flood, the Spirit of the Lord shall lift up a standard against him (Isaiah 59:19).

When thou passest through the waters, I will be with thee; and through the rivers, they shall not overflow thee (Isaiah 43:2a).

Because ye have said, We have made a covenant with death, and with hell are we at agreement; when the overflowing scourge shall pass through, it shall not come unto us: for we have made lies our refuge...the hail shall sweep away the refuge of lies, and the waters shall overflow the hiding place (Isaiah 28:15-17).

FLOWERS—*Glory:* Temporary; gift; romance. **Lily =** *Death;* funeral; mourning. (See ROSE.)

For all flesh is as grass, and all the glory of man as the flower of grass. The grass withereth, and the flower thereof falleth away (1 Peter 1:24).

I am the rose of Sharon, and the lily of the valleys [sorrows and death] *(Song of Solomon 2:1).*

FOG—*Confusion or Temporary:* Clouded issues or thoughts; obscurity; uncertainty.

If I be wicked, woe unto me; and if I be righteous, yet will I not lift up my head. I am full of confusion; therefore see Thou mine affliction (Job 10:15).

O Ephraim, what shall I do unto thee? O Judah, what shall I do unto thee? for your goodness is as a morning cloud [fog], *and as the early dew it goeth away* [is temporary] (Hosea 6:4).

Whereas ye know not what shall be on the morrow. For what is your life? It is even a vapor [fog], *that appeareth for a little time, and then vanisheth away* (James 4:14).

FOOD/MILK—*Work:* **Milk** = *Word of God;* foundational truth; teaching. **Solid Food** = *Work of God.* **Fat** = *Excess;* abundance. (See EATING and MUSHROOMS.)

As newborn babes, desire [to receive] *the sincere milk of the word, that ye may grow thereby* (1 Peter 2:2).

Jesus saith unto them, My meat is to do the will of Him that sent Me, and to finish His work (John 4:34).

For when for the time ye ought to be teachers [workers], *ye have need that one teach you again which be the first principles of the oracles of God; and are become such as have need of milk, and not of strong meat. For every one that useth milk* [is being taught and] *is unskilful in the word of righteousness: for he is a babe* (Hebrews 5:12-13).

The first of the firstfruits of thy land [newborn Christians] *thou shalt bring into the house of the Lord thy God. Thou shalt not seethe* [indoctrinate] *a kid* [babe in Christ] *in his mother's* [church's] *milk* [doctrine, i.e., laws and traditions] (Exodus 23:19).

...All the fat is the Lord's (Leviticus 3:16)

Burn the fat for a sweet savor unto the Lord (Leviticus 17:6b).

FOOTBALL GAME—See PLAY.

FOREIGN MADE (something made oversees, such as a dress, car, or gun)—*Alien:* Not of God; of the flesh; demonic. Not of this world (therefore heavenly). (See NATION, *Section 2*, and FOREIGNER, *Section 7*.)

Our inheritance is turned to strangers [or foreigners], *our houses to aliens* (Lamentations 5:2).

That at that time ye were without Christ, being aliens from the commonwealth of Israel.... Now therefore ye are no more strangers and foreigners, but fellowcitizens... (Ephesians 2:12,19).

Quenched the violence of fire, escaped the edge of the sword, out of weakness were made strong, waxed valiant in fight, turned to flight the armies of the aliens [or foreigners] (Hebrews 11:34).

Jesus answered, My kingdom is not of this world: if My kingdom were of this world, then would My servants fight... (John 18:36).

FOREST—*Foreboding:* Fearful place. **Lost in the Forest** = *Confusion;* without direction. (See TREE.)

Thou makest darkness, and it is night: wherein all the beasts of the forest do creep forth (Psalm 104:20).

They wandered in the wilderness in a solitary way; they found no city to dwell in. Hungry and thirsty, their soul fainted in them (Psalm 107:4-5).

FRUIT—See APPLES.

FURNACE—*Heat Source:* Heart; vengeance; wrath; zeal; anger. (See OVEN.)

My heart was hot within me, while I was musing the fire burned: then spake I with my tongue (Psalm 39:3).

And he looked toward Sodom and Gomorrah…and, lo, the smoke of the country went up as the smoke of a furnace [God's judgment manifest] (Genesis 19:28).

GAMES—See BINGO, CARDS, DOMINOES, and PLAY.

GARBAGE (DUMP)—*Rejected:* Filth; hell; evil; vile; corruption.

And if thine eye offend thee, pluck it out: it is better for thee to enter into the kingdom of God with one eye, than having two eyes to be cast into hell fire [Gk.: "valley of (the son of) Hinnom"; gehenna (i.e., the garbage dump of Jerusalem) used (figuratively) as a name for the place (or state) of everlasting punishment]*: Where their worm dieth not, and the fire is not quenched* (Mark 9:47-48).

But I keep under my body, and bring it into subjection: lest that by any means, when I have preached to others, I myself should be a castaway (1 Corinthians 9:27).

GARDENING—*Working:* Church; ministry (such as a counseling ministry); pleasant pastime. **Garden** = *church;* field of labor. **Vegetables** = *Fruit of one's labor.* (See WEEDS and FLOWERS.)

…And Abel was a keeper of sheep, but Cain was a tiller of the ground. And in process of time it came to pass, that

Cain brought of the fruit of the ground an offering unto the Lord (Genesis 4:2-3).

And the Lord shall guide thee continually, and satisfy thy soul in drought, and make fat thy bones: and thou shalt be like a watered garden, and like a spring of water, whose waters fail not (Isaiah 58:11).

Yet I had planted thee a noble vine, wholly a right seed: how then art thou turned into the degenerate plant of a strange vine unto me? (Jeremiah 2:21)

Neglect not the gift that is in thee, which was given thee by prophecy, with the laying on of the hands of the presbytery. Meditate upon these things; give thyself wholly to them; that thy profiting may appear to all (1 Timothy 4:14-15).

GAS FUMES—*Deception:* Deceiving spirit; evil motive; envy; false accusations; slander; danger; poisonous doctrine.

Be not a witness against thy neighbor without cause; and deceive not with thy lips (Proverbs 24:28).

And Jesus answered and said unto them, Take heed that no man deceive you (Matthew 24:4).

But if ye have bitter envying and strife in your hearts, glory not, and lie not against the truth. This wisdom descendeth not from above, but [ascends from envy and] *is earthly, sensual, devilish* (James 3:14-15).

GASOLINE—*Fuel:* Prayer; inflammatory gossip; contention; strife; danger.

But ye, beloved, building up [refueling] *yourselves on your most holy faith, praying in the Holy Ghost* (Jude 1:20).

Where no wood [fuel] is, there the fire goeth out: so where there is no talebearer, the strife ceaseth. As coals are to burning coals, and wood [or gasoline] to fire; so is a contentious man to kindle strife (Proverbs 26:20-21).

GLOVES—*Covering:* Protection; safe; careful (as in "handle with kid gloves"). **White Gloves** = *Clean;* inspection. **Black or Dirty Gloves** = *Evil works.* (See BLACK, WHITE, *Section 3*, and HANDS, *Section 9*.)

Who shall ascend into the hill of the Lord? or who shall stand in His holy place? He that hath clean hands, and a pure heart; who hath not lifted up his soul unto vanity, nor sworn deceitfully (Psalm 24:3-4).

GOLF—See PLAY.

GRAPES—*Fruit:* The Spirit of promise (Holy Spirit); fruit of the Spirit; promise of wrath. **Pomegranate** = *The Word of God* (because of the seeds).

Ye shall know them by their fruits. Do men gather grapes of thorns...? (Matthew 7:16)

And they came unto the brook of Eshcol, and cut down from thence a branch with one cluster of grapes [the promise of the Holy Spirit (see Eph. 1:13)], *and they bare it between two upon a staff; and they brought of the pomegranates, and of the figs* (Numbers 13:23).

But the fruit of the Spirit is love, joy, peace, longsuffering, gentleness, goodness, faith, meekness, temperance: against such there is no law (Galatians 5:22-23).

GRASS—*Flesh:* Self (as "in the flesh"); the Word of God.

For all flesh is as grass (1 Peter 1:24a).

Ask ye of the Lord rain in the time of the latter rain; so the Lord shall make bright clouds, and give them showers of rain, to every one grass [the revelation of Christ] *in the field* (Zechariah 10:1).

DRIED GRASS—*Death:* Repentance; spiritual drought. (See BROWN, *Section 3.*)

The fourteenth day of the second month at even they shall keep it [the passover], *and eat it with unleavened bread* [sincerity and truth] *and bitter herbs* [a repentant heart] (Numbers 9:11).

My heart is smitten, and withered like grass; so that I forget to eat my bread (Psalm 102:4).

The grass withereth, the flower fadeth: because the spirit of the Lord bloweth upon it [bringing conviction and repentance]: *surely the people is grass. The grass withereth, the flower* [man's glory] *fadeth: but the word of our God shall stand for ever* (Isaiah 40:7-8).

MOWED GRASS—*Chastisement:* Sickness; financial need or distress; emotional and mental depression or anguish. **Mowing Grass** = *Repentance* (as in "crucifying the flesh"); preaching against sin. (See HAY.)

Thus hath the Lord God shown unto me; and, behold, He formed grasshoppers in the beginning of the shooting up of the latter growth; and, lo, it was the latter growth after the king's mowings. And it came to pass, that when they had made an end of eating the grass of the land, then I said, O Lord God, forgive, I beseech thee: by whom shall Jacob arise? for he is small (Amos 7:1-2).

For this cause many are weak and sickly among you, and many sleep [mowed down]. *For if we would judge ourselves, we should not be judged. But when we are judged, we are chastened of the Lord, that we should not be condemned with the world* (1 Corinthians 11:30-32).

GRAVEL PIT—*Source:* The word of God; abundant supply.

A land wherein thou shalt eat bread without scarceness, thou shalt not lack any thing in it; a land whose stones [words] *are iron* [strength], *and out of whose hills thou mayest dig brass* [the Word of God] (Deuteronomy 8:9).

Study [dig] *to show thyself approved unto God, a workman that needeth not to be ashamed, rightly dividing the word of truth* (2 Timothy 2:15).

GRAVEL ROAD—See subheading under HIGHWAY.

GRAVEYARD (or Grave)—*Hidden:* Out of the past; curse; evil inheritance; hypocrisy; death; demon. (See GRANDMOTHER, *Section 7.*)

Woe unto you, scribes and Pharisees, hypocrites! for ye are like unto whited sepulchres, which indeed appear beautiful outward, but are within full of dead men's bones, and of all uncleanness (Matthew 23:27).

Woe unto you, scribes and Pharisees, hypocrites! for ye are as graves which appear not, and the men that walk over them are not aware of them (Luke 11:44).

GUNS/BULLETS—*Words:* Accusations; slander; gossip; power. **Broken or Inoperative Gun** = *Without authority or ability;* without power; hindered. (See BOW/ARROWS.)

That they may shoot in secret at the perfect: suddenly do they shoot at him, and fear not (Psalm 64:4).

When a strong man armed keepeth his palace, his goods are in peace: but when a stronger than he shall come upon him, and overcome him, he taketh from him all his armor wherein he trusted, and divideth his spoils (Luke 11:21-22).

Then certain of the vagabond Jews, exorcists, took upon them[selves, i.e., not authorized by God] *to call over them which had evil spirits the name of the Lord Jesus, saying, We adjure you by Jesus whom Paul preacheth. ... And the evil spirit answered and said, Jesus I know, and Paul I know; but who are ye? And the man in whom the evil spirit was leaped on them, and overcame them, and prevailed against them, so that they fled out of that house naked and wounded* (Acts 19:13,15-16).

.22 CALIBER—*Weak or Ineffective Weapon:* Without power; lack of prayer and fasting.

I know thy works: behold, I have set before thee an open door, and no man can shut it: for thou hast a little strength [or power], *and hast kept My word, and hast not denied My name* (Revelation 3:8).

.357 CALIBER (or other **High Powered Pistol** or **Rifle)—*Powerful:*** Spiritual power through acceptable service; covenant; effective; the power of evil working through agreement (acquiescence) or conquest (our defeat).

For the weapons of our warfare are not carnal, but mighty through God to the pulling down of strong holds (2 Corinthians 10:4).

...Of whom a man is overcome, of the same is he brought in bondage [See Romans 6:16.] (2 Peter 2:19).

HAIL—*Judgment:* Punishment; destruction; bombardment.

> *Judgment also will I lay to the line, and righteousness to the plummet: and the hail shall sweep away the refuge of lies* (Isaiah 28:17a).

> *I smote you with blasting and with mildew and with hail in all the labors of your hands; yet ye turned not to Me, saith the Lord* (Haggai 2:17).

HAIR—*Covering:* Covenant; humanity; the old (sinful) nature; doctrine; tradition. **Long-Haired Man** = *Defiance;* rebellion. **Woman With Long Hair** = *Glorified.* **Shaving** = *Putting away the filthiness or nature of the flesh.* **Haircut** = *Removing or breaking covenants or religious traditions.* **Hair Growing Back Out** = *Restoring the covenant (or tradition).* (See BARBERSHOP, *Section 2.*)

> *But if a woman have long hair, it is a glory to her: for her hair is given her for a covering* (1 Corinthians 11:15).

> *That he told her all his heart, and said unto her, There hath not come a razor upon mine head; for I have been a Nazarite unto God from my mother's womb: if I be shaven* [break the covenant]*, then my strength will go from me, and I shall become weak, and be like any other man* (Judges 16:17).

> *And thus shalt thou do unto them, to cleanse them...let them shave all their flesh* [removing the old nature]*...and so make themselves clean* (Numbers 8:7).

HAMMER—*Force:* Word of God; preaching; evil words; destruction. **Tack Hammer** = *Tactful;* weak. (See NAILS.)

Is not My word like as a fire? saith the Lord; and like a hammer that breaketh the rock [stony heart] *in pieces?* (Jeremiah 23:29)

A man that beareth false witness against his neighbor is a maul [hammer], *and a sword, and a sharp arrow* (Proverbs 25:18).

HANDS—*Works:* Deeds (good or evil); labor; service; idolatry; spiritual warfare. **Raised Hands** = *Worship;* surrender. **Clinched Fist** = *Fighting or anger.* **Two People Shaking Hands** = *Covenant;* agreement. **Hands Trembling** = *Weakness or fear.* **Hands Outstretched, Palms Up** = *Helplessness.* **Hands Covering Face (or Face in One's Hands)** = *Grief;* guilt; shame; laughter. (Other self-explanatory uses of hands include: waving goodbye; begging; prayer (clasped together); calling someone to "come" or to "follow.")

I will therefore that men pray every where, lifting up holy hands, without wrath and doubting (1 Timothy 2:8).

For thou shalt eat the labor of thine hands (Psalm 128:2a).

Give them according to their deeds, and according to the wickedness of their endeavors: give them after the work of their hands... (Psalm 28:4).

Every wise woman buildeth her house: but the foolish plucketh it down with her hands (Proverbs 14:1).

Their idols are silver and gold, the work of men's hands (Psalm 115:4).

Be not thou one of them that strike [shake] *hands, or of them that are sureties for debts* (Proverbs 22:26).

Yea, thou shalt go forth from him [into captivity], *and thine hands upon thine head: for the Lord hath rejected thy confidences, and thou shalt not prosper in them* (Jeremiah 2:37).

HAT—*Covering:* Protection; thought; attitude; activities (as in "wearing many different hats").

For He put on righteousness as a breastplate, and an helmet [the hope] *of salvation upon His head* (Isaiah 59:17a).

HAY—*To Bundle:* Prepare (as in "make hay while the sun shines"); gather people together (as a church) in the name of the Lord but with wrong (selfish) motives; carnality. (See GRASS.)

Now if any man build upon this foundation gold, silver, precious stones, wood, hay, stubble; every man's work shall be made manifest...and the fire shall try every man's work of what sort it is (1 Corinthians 3:12-13).

For all flesh is as grass (1 Peter 1:24a).

HEAD—*Authority:* God; Christ; government; husband; pastor; employer; power.

But I would have you know, that the head of every man is Christ; and the head of the woman is the man; and the head of Christ is God (1 Corinthians 11:3).

Therefore David ran, and stood upon the Philistine, and took his sword...and slew him, and cut off his head therewith. And when the Philistines saw their champion was dead [their power and authority was broken], *they fled* (1 Samuel 17:51).

The hoary [white] *head is a crown of glory, if it be found in the way of righteousness* (Proverbs 16:31).

The ancient and honorable, he is the head (Isaiah 9:15a).

HEAT—See FIRE/HEAT.

HIGHWAY—*Way:* The Christian Faith; truth; way of life (as in "life in the fast lane"); Christ; a person (as in "he knows the way, follow him"); way of error. **Under Construction** = *In Preparation;* change; hindrance. **Crossroads** = *Decision;* change of direction. (See CROSSROADS, PATH, SIGN, and AUTO WRECK, *Section 8.*)

And an highway shall be there, and a way, and it shall be called The way of holiness; the unclean shall not pass over it; but it shall be for those: the wayfaring men, though fools, shall not err therein (Isaiah 35:8).

Enter ye in at the strait gate: for wide is the gate, and broad is the [high]*way, that leadeth to destruction, and many there be which go in thereat: because strait is the gate, and narrow is the* [high]*way, which leadeth unto life, and few there be that find it* (Matthew 7:13-14).

Jesus saith unto him, I am the way... (John 14:6).

The chariots [or automobiles] *shall rage in the streets, they shall jostle one against another* [causing offense] *in the broad ways* [highways that lead to destruction, i.e., worldly churches, false doctrine or sin]: *they shall seem like torches, they shall run like the lightnings* (Nahum 2:4).

DEAD-END ROAD or STREET—*Change Directions:* Stop; repent; certain failure; no advancement possible (as in "that's a dead-end job"); a point at which you must review the way you are going or what you are doing and make the necessary changes in direction.

Now therefore thus saith the Lord of hosts; Consider your ways. Ye have sown much, and bring in little; ye eat, but ye have not enough; ye drink, but ye are not filled with drink; ye clothe you, but there is none warm; and he that earneth wages earneth wages to put it into a bag with holes. Thus saith the Lord of hosts; Consider your ways (Haggai 1:5-7).

GRAVEL ROAD—*Way:* God's Word and way (unless it is muddy, dusty, etc.).

Thus saith the Lord, Stand ye in the ways, and see, and ask for the old paths, where is the good way, and walk therein, and ye shall find rest for your souls (Jeremiah 6:16a).

MUDDY ROAD—*Flesh:* Man's way; lust; passion; temptation; offense; strife; sin; need for caution; impassable; difficulty caused by the weakness of the flesh. **Mud** = *Flesh, in its weakness;* **Ruts** = *Habits or addictions of the flesh;* traditions of man. (See DITCH.)

I sink in deep mire [mud], *where there is no standing* (Psalm 69:2a).

But the wicked are like the troubled sea, when it cannot rest, whose waters cast up mire [mud] *and dirt* (Isaiah 57:20).

Watch and pray, that ye enter not into temptation: the spirit indeed is willing, but the flesh is weak (Matthew 26:41).

HIPS (LOINS)—*Mind:* Truth; joint (as in a relationship "out of joint," i.e., offense between brethren); reproduction.

Wherefore gird up the loins of your mind, be sober... (1 Peter 1:13).

Stand therefore, having your loins girt about with truth... (Ephesians 6:14).

The waters were to the knees. Again he measured a thousand, and brought me through; the waters were to the loins (Ezekiel 47:4b).

For he was yet in the loins of his father, when Melchizedek met him (Hebrews 7:10).

HOMOSEXUAL ACTS—*Against Nature:* **Rebellion; disobedience (i.e., wives not obeying their husbands [witch], husbands not bearing their responsibility of headship properly [wimp]); Also signifies *Abuse of Authority* (leaders using authority for personal gain and fame); fornication when naturally interpreted. (See SEX.)**

For this cause God gave them up unto vile affections: for even their women did change the natural use into that which is against nature [or against the way God made all things in the beginning]. *... And even as they did not like to retain God in their knowledge, God gave them over to a reprobate mind, to do those things which are not convenient; being filled with all unrighteousness, fornication...disobedient to parents* [or husbands] (Romans 1:26,28-30).

Thou art thy mother's daughter, that loatheth [rebelled against] *her husband and her children; and thou art the sister of thy sisters, which loathed their husbands and their children.... Behold, this was the iniquity of thy sister Sodom, pride, fulness of bread, and abundance of idleness was in her and in her daughters, neither did she strengthen the hand of the poor and needy. And they were haughty, and committed abomination before Me…* (Ezekiel 16:45, 49-50).

Let every soul be subject unto the higher powers. For there is no power but of God: the powers that be are ordained of God [and therefore God given authority should not be misused] (Romans 13:1).

Thou shalt not lie with mankind, as with womankind: it is abomination (Leviticus 18:22).

HONEY—*Strength:* Power; Holy Spirit anointing and enlightenment; wisdom; knowledge; pleasant experience.

And he said unto them, Out of the eater came forth meat, and out of the strong [Christ] *came forth sweetness…* [honey, i.e., strength (see Rom. 5:6)] (Judges 14:14).

A wise man is strong; yea, a man of knowledge increaseth strength (Proverbs 24:5).

The full soul loatheth an honeycomb; but to the hungry soul every bitter thing is sweet (Proverbs 27:7).

Then said Jonathan, My father hath troubled the land: see, I pray you, how mine eyes have been enlightened, because I tasted a little of this honey (1 Samuel 14:29).

HORNS—*Authority:* Power; ability; kings; anointing (anointing oil was carried in a horn).

All the horns [authority and ability] *of the wicked also will I cut off; but the horns of the righteous shall be exalted* (Psalm 75:10).

God is the Lord, which hath shown us light: bind the sacrifice with cords [vows], *even unto the horns* [power and authority, i.e., unto Christ (see 1 Cor. 1:24)] *of the altar* (Psalm 118:27).

Because ye have thrust with side and with shoulder, and pushed all the diseased with your horns, till ye have scattered them abroad [misuse of authority] (Ezekiel 34:21).

And the ten horns which thou sawest are ten kings... (Revelation 17:12).

HUNTING—See WILD GAME, *Section 1.*

ICE—See SNOW/ICE.

INSURANCE—*Faith:* Protection; prepared; safe; covered; confidence; future provision for one's family.

The God of my rock; in Him will I trust: He is my shield, and the horn of my salvation, my high tower, and my refuge, my savior; Thou savest me from violence (2 Samuel 22:3).

INTERSECTION—See HIGHWAY.

IRONING—*Correction:* Change; sanctification; exhortation; instruction in righteousness; God's discipline; repentance; working out problem relationships; reconciliation (as in "ironing out differences"); pressure (from trials).

That He might present it to Himself a glorious church, not having spot, or wrinkle, or any such thing; but that it should be holy and without blemish (Ephesians 5:27).

JEWELRY—*Treasure:* Desire; precious; God's gifts; idolatry; self-glorification; pride. **Jewel** = *Precious person;* gifted person; truth. (See SILVER, GOLD, *Section 5,* DIAMOND and RING, *Section 9.*)

For the time will come when they will not endure sound doctrine; but after their own lusts shall they heap to themselves teachers, having itching ears [desire for doctrines that justify or please the lust of the flesh; compare Matthew 6:21: "For where your treasure is, there will your heart be also"] *(2 Timothy 4:3).*

A gift is as a precious stone in the eyes of him that hath it: whithersoever it turneth, it prospereth (Proverbs 17:8).

For if there come unto your assembly a man with a gold ring [self-glorification], *in goodly apparel* (James 2:2a).

As a jewel of gold in a swine's snout, so is a fair woman which is without discretion (Proverbs 11:22).

JOGGING—See RUNNING.

KEY—*Knowledge:* Authority; wisdom; understanding; ability; important or indispensable (as in "the key man"); Christ.

Woe unto you, lawyers! for ye have taken away the key of knowledge (Luke 11:52a).

All things were made by Him; and without Him was not any thing made that was made (John 1:3).

And I have filled him with the spirit of God, in wisdom, and in understanding, and in knowledge, and in all manner of workmanship (Exodus 31:3).

KICKING—See FEET.

KISS—*Agreement:* Covenant; enticement; betrayal; covenant breaker; deception; seduction; friend. (See SEX.)

Kiss the Son, lest He be angry, and ye perish from the way, when His wrath is kindled but a little... (Psalm 2:12).

Faithful are the wounds of a friend; but the kisses of an enemy are deceitful (Proverbs 27:6).

But Jesus said unto him, Judas, betrayest thou the Son of man with a kiss? (Luke 22:48)

And Joab said to Amasa, Art thou in health, my brother? And Joab took Amasa by the beard with the right hand to kiss him. But Amasa took no heed to the sword that was in Joab's hand: so he smote him therewith in the fifth rib...and he died... (2 Samuel 20:9-10).

And, behold, there met him a woman with the attire of an harlot, and subtle of heart. ... So she caught him, and kissed him.... He goeth after her straightway, as an ox goeth to the slaughter, or as a fool to the correction of the stocks...and knoweth not that it is for his life. ... Her house is the way to hell, going down to the chambers of death (Proverbs 7:10,13,22-23,27).

KNEES—*Submission:* Obey; worship; serve; stubborn; unyielding. (See ANKLES, HIPS.)

But what saith the answer of God unto him? I have reserved to myself seven thousand men, who have not bowed the knee to the image of Baal (Romans 11:4).

For it is written, As I live, saith the Lord, every knee shall bow to Me, and every tongue shall confess to God (Romans 14:11).

Again he measured a thousand, and brought me through the waters; the waters were to the knees [submission to God's Spirit] (Ezekiel 47:4a).

KNIVES—*Words:* Revelation; truth; sharp or angry rebuke; accusations; gossip. **Pocket Knife** = *Personal revelation of practical use or value.* (See SWORD.)

Thy tongue deviseth mischiefs; like a sharp razor, working deceitfully (Psalm 52:2).

This witness is true. Wherefore rebuke them sharply [cut them off], *that they may be sound in the faith* (Titus 1:13).

LADDER—*Ascend or Descend:* Enable; way of escape; way of entrance; struggle (if hard to climb); steps upward (as in "the necessary steps for a promotion"). **Fireman's Ladder** = *Rescue;* help. (See STAIRS.)

And he dreamed, and behold a ladder set up on the earth, and the top of it reached to heaven: and behold the angels of God ascending and descending on it. And, behold, the Lord stood above it, and said...the land whereon thou liest, to thee will I give it, and to thy seed (Genesis 28:12-13).

And no man hath ascended [climbed] *up to heaven, but he that came down from heaven, even the Son of man which is in heaven* (John 3:13).

LEMON—*Sour:* Bad deal (as in "that car we bought is a lemon"); crabby.

They gave Him vinegar to drink mingled with gall: and when He had tasted thereof, He would not drink (Matthew 27:34).

For I perceive that thou art in the gall of bitterness, and in the bond of iniquity (Acts 8:23).

LEAVEN—*Spirit (Good or Evil):* Attitude; sin; false doctrine; hypocrisy; self-justification; self-righteousness; self-importance; anger; pride; zeal.

Therefore let us keep the feast, not with old leaven, neither with the leaven of malice and wickedness; but with the unleavened bread of sincerity and truth (1 Corinthians 5:8).

And He charged them, saying, Take heed, beware of the leaven of the Pharisees [hypocrisy (see Lk. 12:1), and self-righteousness (see Mt. 16:6,12], *and of the leaven of Herod* [pride and the abuse of authority (see Mt. 2:13; 14:6-9)] (Mark 8:15).

Your glorying [pride, boasting, self-importance] *is not good. Know ye not that a little leaven leaveneth the whole lump?* (1 Corinthians 5:6)

LEAVES—*Words or Life:* Covering; covenant; testimony; doctrine; temporary; self-justification.

And the eyes of them both were opened, and they knew that they were naked; and they sewed fig leaves together [self-justification], *and made themselves aprons* (Genesis 3:7).

But we are all as an unclean thing...and we all do fade as a leaf; and our iniquities, like the wind, have taken us away (Isaiah 64:6).

And when He saw a fig tree in the way, He came to it, and found nothing thereon, but leaves only [words without corresponding works], *and said unto it, Let no fruit grow on thee henceforward for ever. And presently the fig tree withered away* (Matthew 21:19).

In the midst of the street of it, and on either side of the river, was there the tree of life...and the leaves of the tree were for the healing of the nations (Revelation 22:2).

LEGS—*Support:* Spirit; strength. **Female Legs** = *Seduction* (see THIGH; for **Shaving Legs**, see HAIR).

He delighteth not in the strength of the horse: he taketh not pleasure in the legs [strength] *of a man* (Psalm 147:10).

The legs of the lame are not equal: so is a parable in the mouth of fools [i.e., does not support or relate to his doctrine] (Proverbs 26:7).

The spirit of a man will sustain [or support] *his infirmity; but a wounded* [or broken] *spirit who can bear?* (Proverbs 18:14)

LIGHT—*Manifest:* Revealed; exposed. **Lights Turned Off** = *Without understanding or manifestation.* **Flashlight** = *Personal knowledge or understanding;* guidance. **Dim Light** = *Without full knowledge or understanding.*

But all things that are reproved are made manifest by the light: for whatsoever doth make manifest is light (Ephesians 5:13).

But he that doeth truth cometh to the light, that his deeds may be made manifest, that they are wrought in God (John 3:21).

And there were many lights in the upper chamber, where they were gathered together [openly, not in secret] (Acts 20:8).

Thy word is a lamp unto my feet, and a light unto my path (Psalm 119:105).

LIGHTNING—*Power:* Instant miracle; judgment; destruction; knowledge. (See THUNDER and ELECTRICITY.)

And the seventy returned again with joy, saying, Lord, even the devils are subject unto us through Thy name. And He said unto them, [when you cast them out] *I beheld Satan as lightning fall from heaven* [i.e., by God's miraculous power] (Luke 10:17-18).

Cast forth lightning, and scatter them: shoot out thine arrows, and destroy them (Psalm 144:6).

LIPS—*Words:* Seduction; speech. (See KISS and PEN/PENCIL.)

With her much fair speech she caused him to yield, with the flattering of her lips she forced [persuaded or seduced] *him* (Proverbs 7:21).

In the multitude of words there wanteth not sin: but he that refraineth his lips is wise (Proverbs 10:19).

LOST AND FOUND—*Lose/Gain:* **Lost** = *Truth lost through tradition;* gift lost through neglect; soul lost through sin. **Found** = *Revelations or gifts received from God.* **Finding Silver Coins or Knives** = *Receiving revelation knowledge.* (See SILVER, *Section 5,* and KNIVES, *Section 9.*)

Beware lest any man spoil you [cause you to lose the truth] *through philosophy and vain deceit, after the tradition of men, after the rudiments of the world, and not after Christ* (Colossians 2:8).

When they were filled, He said unto His disciples, Gather up the fragments that remain, that nothing be lost (John 6:12).

Thy words were found, and I did eat [partake of them, i.e., obey] *them; and Thy word was unto me the joy and rejoicing of mine heart* (Jeremiah 15:16a).

LUMBER—See WOOD.

MACHINES—*Work or Motion:* Idle words; productivity. (See FACTORY, *Section 2.*)

Lo, this only have I found, that God hath made man upright; but they have sought out many inventions (Ecclesiastes 7:29).

But I say unto you, That every idle word that men shall speak, they shall give account thereof in the day of judgment (Matthew 12:36).

For when we were in the flesh, the motions of sins [like a motor running], *which were by the law, did work in our members to bring forth fruit unto death* (Romans 7:5).

MAP—*Directions:* Word of God; correction; advice.

For the commandment is a lamp; and the law is light; and reproofs of instruction are the way [or map] *of life* (Proverbs 6:23).

MARRIAGE—*Covenant:* The Church as the Bride of Christ; agreement; joined. **Sexual Intimacy** = *One in agreement.* **Interruption of Intimacy** = *Interference or trouble in the marriage or covenant relationship.* (See SEX.) Natural marriage when naturally interpreted.

For this cause shall a man leave his father and mother, and shall be joined unto his wife, and they two shall be one flesh. This is a great mystery: but I speak concerning Christ and the church (Ephesians 5:31-32).

Shall we then hearken unto you to do all this great evil, to transgress against our God in marrying strange wives [of making covenants with those who are not in agreement with God (see Ex. 23:32; 2 Cor. 6:14)]*?* (Nehemiah 13:27)

And to the angel of the church in Pergamos [Gk.: "much marriage," i.e., covenants of sin, therefore much worldliness] *write...* (Revelation 2:12).

MEDICINE—See DRUGS.

MICROPHONE—*Voice:* Authority; ministry; influence.

What I tell you in darkness, that speak ye in light: and what ye hear in the ear, that preach ye upon the housetops (Matthew 10:27).

MICROSCOPE—*Examine:* Close examination; self-examination; discern (as in discerning of spirits).

But let a man examine himself, and so let him eat of that bread, and drink of that cup (1 Corinthians 11:28).

MICROWAVE OVEN—*Instant:* Quick work; sudden; impatience; convenience.

For he will finish the work, and cut it short in righteousness: because a short work will the Lord make upon the earth (Romans 9:28).

MILK—See FOOD/MILK.

MIRROR—*God's Word or One's Heart:* Looking at oneself; looking back; memory; past; vanity; Moses' Law. (See REARVIEW MIRROR, *Section 8.*)

For now we see through a glass [Moses' Law, which is as a mirror], *darkly* [in dark sayings, or parables]*; but then face to face: now I know in part; but then shall I know even as also I am known* (1 Corinthians 13:12).

As in water [or a mirror] *face answereth to face, so the heart of man to man* [Compare Romans 2:1: "Therefore thou art inexcusable, O man, whosoever thou art that judgest: for wherein thou judgest another, thou condemnest thyself; for thou that judgest doest the same things."] (Proverbs 27:19).

MISCARRIAGE—*Abort:* Failure; loss; repentance; unjust judgment (as in "miscarriage of justice").

Give them, O Lord: what wilt Thou give? give them a mis-carrying womb and dry breasts (Hosea 9:14).

Then when lust hath conceived, it bringeth forth sin: and sin, when it is finished, bringeth forth death [unless repentance (miscarriage) stops the process. Compare Psalm 7:14: "Behold, he travaileth with iniquity, and hath conceived mischief, and brought forth falsehood."] (James 1:15).

Therefore the law is slacked, and judgment doth never go forth: for the wicked doth compass about the righteous; therefore wrong judgment proceedeth (Habakkuk 1:4).

MISSILE—See ROCKET.

MONEY—*Power:* Provision; wealth; natural talents and skills; spiritual riches (i.e., faith, wisdom, spiritual gifts, etc.); power; authority; the strength of man (as opposed to trusting in God); covetousness.

But thou shalt remember the Lord thy God: for it is He that giveth thee power to get wealth... (Deuteronomy 8:18).

Are we not counted of him strangers? for he hath sold us, and hath quite devoured also our money [wealth, health, etc.] (Genesis 31:15).

Wherefore then gavest not thou my money [talents, spiritual gifts, etc.] *into the bank* [submitted to those God has placed in authority], *that at my coming I might have required mine own with usury?* (Luke 19:23)

For the love of money is the root of all evil: which while some coveted after, they have erred from the faith, and pierced themselves through with many sorrows (1 Timothy 6:10).

The inhabitants of Samaria shall fear because of the calves of Bethaven [Heb.: "House of Vanity," i.e., as opposed to Bethel, the house of God]: *for the people thereof shall mourn over it* [because of the economic depression brought on the land because of the sin of covetousness], *and the priests thereof that rejoiced on it, for the glory thereof, because it is departed from it* [See Jeremiah 7:8-11.] (Hosea 10:5).

For wisdom is a defense, and money is a [man's] *defense: but the excellency of knowledge is, that wisdom giveth life to them that have it* (Ecclesiastes 7:12).

If therefore ye have not been faithful in the unrighteous mammon, who will commit to your trust the true riches? (Luke 16:11)

MOON—*Church (true or apostate):* To rule; to manifest the works of darkness; occult; false worship. **Moon as Blood** = *Persecution.* (See SUN.)

And God made two great lights; the greater light to rule the day [**Sun** = *Christ*], *and the lesser light to rule the night* [**Moon** = *Church*]: *He made the stars also* (Genesis 1:16).

Blessed be the God and Father of our Lord Jesus Christ, who hath blessed us with all spiritual blessings in heavenly places [as the moon is in the heavens] *in Christ* (Ephesians 1:3).

And for the precious fruits brought forth by the sun [see 1 Cor. 3:6], *and for the precious things* [salvation] *put forth by the moon* [Church] (Deuteronomy 33:14).

Moreover the light of the moon [Church] *shall be as the light of the sun* [Christ]*, and the light of the sun* [Christ] *shall be sevenfold* [complete, nothing hidden], *as the light of seven days, in the day that the Lord bindeth up the breach of His people, and healeth the stroke of their wound* (Isaiah 30:26).

But in those days, after that tribulation, the sun shall be darkened, and the moon [Church] *shall not give her light* [darkness, as in John 9:4b, "The night cometh, when no man can work."] (Mark 13:24).

The sun shall be turned into darkness, and the moon into blood [Church persecuted], *before that great and notable day of the Lord come* (Acts 2:20).

And he put down the idolatrous priests...that burned incense unto Baal, to the sun, and to the moon...and to all the host of heaven (2 Kings 23:5).

MOUNTAIN—*Exalted:* Obstacle; difficulty; challenge; kingdom (nation).

Now therefore give me this mountain, whereof the Lord spake in that day; for thou heardest in that day how the Anakims [giants] *were there, and that the cities were great and fenced* (Joshua 14:12a).

And the heaven departed as a scroll when it is rolled together; and every mountain [nation] *and island* [independent country] *were moved out of their places* [shift of the balance of power, economic, military, political, etc.] (Revelation 6:14).

MOVIE—See PICTURE.

MOVING (as in changing churches, jobs, houses, etc.)—*Change:* (See HOUSE, subheading NEW HOUSE, *Section 2.*)

Therefore, thou son of man, prepare thee stuff for removing, and remove by day in their sight; and thou shalt remove from thy place to another place in their sight (Ezekiel 12:3a).

MUD (Muddy Road, Path, or River)—See HIGHWAY, DITCH, and RIVER.

MUSHROOM—*Quick:* Sudden growth; sudden or unexpected appearance; fragile; deadly poison.

Then said the Lord, Thou hast had pity on the gourd, for the which thou hast not labored, neither madest it grow; which came up in a night [like a mushroom], and perished in a night (Jonah 4:10).

I have declared the former things from the beginning; and they went forth out of my mouth, and I showed them; I did them suddenly, and they came to pass (Isaiah 48:3).

MUSIC—*Worship:* Of God; of idols (idolatry); activity or action that proceeds from the heart. **Playing Instruments** = *Prophesying;* ministering in the gifts of the Spirit; worshiping. (See TRUMPET.)

And, lo, Thou art unto them as a very lovely song of one that hath a pleasant voice, and can play well on an instrument: for they hear Thy words, but they do them not (Ezekiel 33:32).

That at what time ye hear the sound of the cornet, flute, harp, sackbut, psaltery, dulcimer, and all kinds of music, ye fall down and worship the golden image that Nebuchadnezzar the king hath set up (Daniel 3:5).

NAILS—*Words:* Word of God or man; wisdom; vows; covenant; fasten; steadfast; permanent; unmovable; unchangeable; secure (as in "they stole everything that wasn't nailed down"). (See HAMMER.)

The words of the wise are as goads, and as nails fastened by the masters of assemblies, which are given from one shepherd (Ecclesiastes 12:11).

So the carpenter encouraged the goldsmith, and he that smootheth with the hammer him that smote the anvil, saying, It [the idol] *is ready for the sodering: and he fastened it with nails* [words (doctrines, vows, or covenant promises)], *that it should not be moved* (Isaiah 41:7).

NAME—*Identity:* Authority; reputation; the name's meaning (for example, **Jill** means "youthful"); a person whose name rhymes with the name in the dream; a person with the same initials; a different person with the same name or similar personality, nature, character, or reputation; the actual person in the dream. (See FRIEND, *Section 7.*)

Then said God, Call his name Lo-ammi [Heb.: "Not My people"]: *for ye are not My people, and I will not be your God* (Hosea 1:9).

And they said, Go to, let us build us a city and a tower, whose top may reach unto heaven; and let us make us a name [reputation], *lest we be scattered abroad upon the face of the whole earth* (Genesis 11:4).

NECK—*Will:* Self-willed; stubborn; unbelief; authority; rule.

But they obeyed not, neither inclined their ear, but made their neck stiff, that they might not hear, nor receive instruction (Jeremiah 17:23).

And Pharaoh took off his ring from his hand, and put it upon Joseph's hand...and put a gold chain about his neck (Genesis 41:42).

NEWSPAPER—*Announcement:* Important event; public exposure; news; prophecy; gossip.

For nothing is secret, that shall not be made manifest; neither any thing hid, that shall not be known and come abroad (Luke 8:17).

NIGHT—*Darkness:* Ignorance; hidden; unknown course of action; sin; power of evil; stealth (as in "they crept in under cover of darkness").

But if a man walk in the night, he stumbleth [sins], because there is no light in him (John 11:10).

Then Jesus said unto them, Yet a little while is the light with you. Walk while ye have the light, lest darkness come upon you: for he that walketh in darkness knoweth not whither he goeth (John 12:35).

When I was daily with you in the temple, ye stretched forth no hands against me: but this is your hour, and the power of darkness (Luke 22:53).

For they that sleep sleep in the night; and they that be drunken are drunken in the night (1 Thessalonians 5:7).

NOISE—*Annoyance:* Interference (like static interferes with proper radio reception). **Loud Noise** = *Alarm;* sudden fright.

And when Joshua heard the noise of the people as they shouted, he said unto Moses, There is a noise of war in the camp (Exodus 32:17).

It is better to dwell in the wilderness, than with a contentious and an angry woman (Proverbs 21:19).

NOSE—*Busybody or Discern:* Nosy (as in "sticking your nose into other people's business"); meddling; strife; smell (discern). **Nosebleed** = *Strife;* trouble.

But let none of you suffer as a murderer, or as a thief, or as an evildoer, or as a busybody in other men's matters [being nosy] (1 Peter 4:15).

Surely...the wringing of the nose bringeth forth blood: so the forcing of wrath bringeth forth strife (Proverbs 30:33).

They have ears, but they hear not: noses have they, but they smell not (Psalm 115:6).

NUDITY—*Uncovered or Flesh:* In (or of) the flesh; self-justification and self-righteousness (not under grace, see Galatians 5:4); impure; ashamed; stubborn; temptation; lust; using sex to control others (which is witchcraft); exhibitionism; innocence (as in "a nude baby or child"); open (i.e., revealed); truth; honest; nature.

Because thou sayest, I am rich, and increased with goods, and have need of nothing; and knowest not that thou art wretched, and miserable, and poor, and blind, and naked (Revelation 3:17).

Behold, I come as a thief. Blessed is he that watcheth, and keepeth his garments, lest he walk naked, and they see his shame (Revelation 16:15).

Therefore the showers have been withholden, and there hath been no latter rain; and thou hadst a whore's forehead [stubborn], thou refusedst to be ashamed (Jeremiah 3:3).

And he stripped off his clothes also, and prophesied before Samuel in like manner, and lay down naked all that day and all that night (1 Samuel 19:24a).

And they were both naked, the man and his wife, and were not ashamed (Genesis 2:25).

NUTS AND BOLTS—*Essential:* Bottom line (as in "getting down to the real nuts and bolts of an issue");

indispensable; wisdom; to fasten. **Lock Washer** = *Secure;* unmovable; unyielding.

Wisdom is the principal [essential] *thing; therefore get wisdom: and with all thy getting get understanding* (Proverbs 4:7).

OIL—*Anointing:* **Clear Oil** = *Holy Spirit anointing;* healing. **Dirty Oil** = *Unclean spirit;* hate; lust; seduction; deception; slick (slippery); danger of slipping.

Is any sick among you? let him call for the elders of the church; and let them pray over him, anointing him with oil in the name of the Lord (James 5:14).

But the wise took oil [the Holy Spirit] *in their vessels with their lamps* (Matthew 25:4).

The words of his mouth were smoother than butter, but war was in his heart: his words were softer than oil, yet were they drawn swords (Psalm 55:21).

For the lips of a strange woman drop as an honeycomb, and her mouth is smoother than oil (Proverbs 5:3).

OVEN—*Heart:* Heat of passion; one's imagination "cooking up" good or evil; meditation; judgment. (See BAKER, *Section 7,* KITCHEN, *Section 2,* FURNACE and FIRE/HEAT, *Section 9.*)

For they have made ready their heart like an oven, whiles they lie in wait: their baker sleepeth all the night; in the morning it burneth as a flaming fire [consumed with passion] (Hosea 7:6).

Thou shalt make them as a fiery oven in the time of Thine anger: the Lord shall swallow them up in His wrath, and the fire shall devour them [make them as a burned cake] (Psalm 21:9).

But if they cannot contain, let them marry: for it is better to marry than to burn [with lust] (1 Corinthians 7:9).

PAINTING—*Covering:* Regenerate; remodel; renovate; love. **House Painter's Brush** = *Ministry or minister.* **Painting** = *Preaching;* covering up (hiding) sin. **Paint** = *Doctrine;* truth or deception. **Artist's Painting** = *Words;* illustrative message; eloquent; humorous; articulate. (See *Section 3* for colors.)

And above all things have fervent charity among yourselves: for charity [is the paint which] *shall cover the multitude of sins* (1 Peter 4:8).

Woe unto you, scribes and Pharisees, hypocrites! for ye are like unto whited [painted] *sepulchres, which indeed appear beautiful outward, but are within full of dead men's bones, and of all uncleanness* (Matthew 23:27).

Not by works of righteousness which we have done, but according to His mercy He saved us, by the washing of regeneration, and renewing of the Holy Ghost (Titus 3:5).

And a certain Jew named Apollos, born at Alexandria, an eloquent man [like an skillful artist], *and mighty in the scriptures, came to Ephesus* (Acts 18:24).

PARACHUTING—*Leave:* Bail out; escape; flee; saved. **Parachute** = *God's promises;* salvation; faith.

But when they persecute you in this city, flee ye into another... (Matthew 10:23).

PATH—*Way:* Life; private walk with God; gospel; salvation; error; misjudgment. (See HIGHWAY.)

Thus saith the Lord, Stand ye in the ways, and see, and ask for the old paths, where is the good way, and walk therein, and ye shall find rest for your souls... (Jeremiah 6:16).

Wherefore I was grieved with that generation, and said, They do always err in their heart; and they have not known My ways (Hebrews 3:10).

PEN/PENCIL—*Tongue:* Indelible words; covenant; agreement; contract; vow; publish; record; permanent; unforgettable; gossip.

My heart is inditing a good matter...my tongue is the pen of a ready writer (Psalm 45:1).

For thou writest bitter things against me, and makest me to possess the iniquities of my youth (Job 13:26).

How do ye say, We are wise, and the law of the Lord is with us? Lo, certainly in vain made he it; the pen [word] of the scribes is in vain [See Jeremiah 17:1.] (Jeremiah 8:8).

PERFUME—*Influence:* Seduction; enticement; temptation; persuasion; deception.

I discerned among the youths, a young man void of understanding. ... And, behold, there met him a woman with the attire of an harlot, and subtle of heart. ... So she caught him, and kissed him, and with an impudent face said unto him ... I have perfumed my bed with myrrh, aloes, and cinnamon. Come, let us take our fill of love until the morning... (Proverbs 7:7b,10,13,17-18).

Dead flies cause the ointment of the apothecary to send forth a stinking savor: so doth a little folly him that is in reputation for wisdom and honor (Ecclesiastes 10:1).

PICTURE—*Memory:* Conscience; past experience; circumstance; imagination; a message within itself (as in "a picture is worth a thousand words"). **Picture Taken With an Important Person** = *Honor;* promotion. **Unusual Picture Frame** = *Attitude* (as in "a peculiar frame of mind"); **Old or Antique Frame** = *Time or age* (as in "memories from the past").

> *Then ye shall drive out all the inhabitants of the land from before you, and destroy all their pictures* [pornography, etc.]*, and destroy all their molten images, and quite pluck down all their high places* [See Isaiah 2:11-12,16.] (Numbers 33:52).

> *How much more shall the blood of Christ...purge your conscience* [both conscious and unconscious memories with the associated guilt] *from dead works to serve the living God?* (Hebrews 9:14)

PIE—*Whole:* Business endeavors (as in "having a finger in a lot of pies"); part of the action (as in "I'd like a piece of that pie, myself"). For **Fruit Pie**, see APPLES. Also see PUMPKIN.

> *And one of the company said unto Him, Master, speak to my brother, that he divide the inheritance with me* (Luke 12:13).

PILLS—See DRUGS.

PIPE—See SMOKING.

PISTOL—See GUNS/BULLETS.

PLATE—See POT/PAN/BOWL.

PLAY—*Worship:* Idolatry; covetousness; true worship; spiritual warfare; striving; competition. (See MUSIC, DANCING.)

Neither be ye idolaters, as were some of them; as it is written, The people sat down to eat and drink, and rose up to play [See Exodus 32:19.] (1 Corinthians 10:7).

Mortify therefore your members which are upon the earth; fornication, uncleanness, inordinate affection, evil concupiscence, and covetousness, which is idolatry (Colossians 3:5).

Know ye not that they which run in a race [or play a competitive game] *run all, but one receiveth the prize? So run* [or strive, fight, etc.], *that ye may obtain* (1 Corinthians 9:24).

POMEGRANATE—See GRAPES.

POND—See SWIMMING POOL.

POSTAGE STAMP—*Seal:* Authority; authorization; small or seemingly insignificant, but powerful.

...The writing which is written in the king's name, and sealed with the king's ring, may no man reverse (Esther 8:8).

Labor not for the meat which perisheth, but for that meat which endureth unto everlasting life, which the Son of man shall give unto you: for Him hath God the Father sealed [given authority] (John 6:27).

POT/PAN/BOWL—*Vessel:* Doctrine; tradition; a determination or resolve; form of the truth; a person.

An instructor of the foolish, a teacher of babes, which hast the form [container] *of knowledge and of the truth in the law* (Romans 2:20).

And thou shalt make the dishes thereof, and spoons [precepts] *thereof, and covers* [spirit] *thereof, and bowls* [doctrines] *thereof, to cover* [the people] *withal: of pure gold*

[God's wisdom] *shalt thou make them* [See Isaiah 28:9-10 and GOLD, *Section 5.*] (Exodus 25:29).

And the word of the Lord came unto me the second time, saying, What seest thou? And I said, I see a seething pot [angry determination]; *and the face thereof is toward the north* [judgment] (Jeremiah 1:13).

And I will stretch over Jerusalem the line of Samaria, and the plummet of the house of Ahab: and I will wipe Jerusalem as a man wipeth a dish, wiping it, and turning it upside down (2 Kings 21:13).

For this is the will of God, even your sanctification, that ye should abstain from fornication: that every one of you should know how to possess his vessel [body or wife] *in sanctification and honor; not in the lust of concupiscence, even as the Gentiles which know not God* (1 Thessalonians 4:3-5).

PREGNANCY—*In Process:* Sin or righteousness in process; desire; anticipation; expectancy. **Labor Pains** = *Trials.* (See BABY.)

Shall I bring to the birth, and not cause to bring forth? saith the Lord: shall I cause to bring forth, and shut the womb? saith thy God (Isaiah 66:9).

Then when lust hath conceived, it bringeth forth sin: and sin, when it is finished, bringeth forth death [Compare Psalm 7:14: "Behold, he travaileth with iniquity, and hath conceived mischief, and brought forth falsehood."] (James 1:15).

For nation shall rise against nation, and kingdom against kingdom: and there shall be earthquakes in divers places, and there shall be famines and troubles: these are the beginnings of sorrows [Gk.: "throes of childbirth"] (Mark 13:8).

PUMPKIN—*Witchcraft:* Deception; snare; witch; trick (as in "Halloween trick-or-treat").

For they intended evil against thee; they imagined a mischievous device, which they are not able to perform (Psalm 21:11).

PURSE (or Wallet)—Treasure: Heart; personal identity; precious; valuable; when empty, spiritually bankrupt. (See BANK, *Section 2.*)

For where your treasure is [purse, wallet, bank account, or precious possessions], *there will your heart be also* (Matthew 6:21).

A good man out of the good treasure of the heart bringeth forth good things: and an evil man out of the evil treasure bringeth forth evil things (Matthew 12:35).

This he said, not that he cared for the poor; but because he was a thief, and had the bag [purse], *and bare what was put therein* (John 12:6).

RADIO (SOUND)—*Unceasing:* Continuous; unrelenting; contentious; unbelieving; tradition; news; the gospel being broadcast.

A foolish woman is clamorous [talking continually]*: she is simple, and knoweth nothing* (Proverbs 9:13).

A continual dropping in a very rainy day and a contentious woman are alike (Proverbs 27:15).

RADIO TOWER—*Broadcast:* Truth or error; gospel; witness.

And this gospel of the kingdom shall be preached [broadcast] *in all the world for a witness unto all nations; and then shall the end come* (Matthew 24:14).

RAILROAD TRACK—*Tradition:* Unchanging; habit; stubborn; gospel; caution (as in "stop, look, and listen"); danger. (See TRAIN, *Section 8.*)

And He said unto them, Full well ye reject the commandment of God, that ye may keep your own tradition. ... Making the word of God of none effect through your tradition... (Mark 7:9,13).

Beware lest any man spoil you through philosophy and vain deceit, after the tradition of men, after the rudiments of the world, and not after Christ (Colossians 2:8).

Therefore, brethren, stand fast, and hold the traditions [stay on the established track] *which ye have been taught.... Now we command you, brethren, in the name of our Lord Jesus Christ, that ye withdraw yourselves from every brother that walketh disorderly, and not after the tradition which he received of us* (2 Thessalonians 2:15; 3:6).

RAIN—*Life:* Revival; Holy Spirit; Word of God; depression; trial; disappointment (as in "raining on someone's parade"). **Drought** = *Blessings withheld* (because of sin); without God's presence.

Ask ye of the Lord rain in the time of the latter rain; so the Lord shall make bright clouds, and give them showers of rain, to every one grass in the field (Zechariah 10:1).

For as the rain cometh down, and the snow from heaven, and returneth not thither, but watereth the earth, and maketh it bring forth and bud, that it may give seed to the sower, and bread to the eater: so shall My word be that goeth forth out of My mouth: it shall not return unto Me void, but it shall accomplish that which I please… (Isaiah 55:10-11).

And the rain descended, and the floods came, and the winds blew, and beat upon that house [of the unwise man]*; and it fell: and great was the fall of it* (Matthew 7:27).

Therefore the showers have been withholden, and there hath been no latter rain; and thou hadst a whore's forehead, thou refusedst to be ashamed (Jeremiah 3:3).

RAINBOW—*Covenant:* Promise; good; protection.

I do set My bow in the cloud, and it shall be for a token of a covenant between Me and the earth (Genesis 9:13).

RAPE—*Violating Another's Will:* Violation; abuse of authority; hate; desire for revenge; murder. (See SEX.)

And she answered him, Nay, my brother, do not force me…do not thou this folly. … Howbeit he would not hearken unto her voice: but, being stronger than she, forced her, and lay with her. Then Amnon hated her exceedingly; so that the hatred wherewith he hated her was greater than the love wherewith he had loved her. And Amnon said unto her, Arise, be gone (2 Samuel 13:12,14-15).

But if a man find a betrothed damsel in the field, and the man force her, and lie with her: then the man only that lay with her shall die: but unto the damsel thou shalt do nothing; there is in the damsel no sin worthy of death: for as when a man riseth against his neighbor, and slayeth him [murder]*, even so is this matter* (Deuteronomy 22:25-26).

RAPTURE—*Revival (Personal or concerning the Church):* Spiritual awakening; warning of unpreparedness if left behind!

After two days will He revive us: in the third day He will raise us up, and we shall live in His sight (Hosea 6:2).

O Lord, I have heard Thy speech, and was afraid: O Lord, revive Thy work in the midst of the years, in the midst of the years make known; in wrath remember mercy (Habakkuk 3:2).

REED—*Weak:* A spiritually weak person; opposition that comes through the weakness of the flesh; affliction (when used as a whip).

Now, behold, thou trustest upon the staff of this bruised reed, even upon Egypt, on which if a man lean, it will go into his hand, and pierce it: so is Pharaoh king of Egypt unto all that trust on him (2 Kings 18:21).

Watch and pray, that ye enter not into temptation: the spirit indeed is willing, but the flesh is weak (Matthew 26:41).

REFRIGERATOR—*Heart:* Motive; attitude; thoughts. **Stored Food** = *Memories stored in the heart;* **Spoiled Food** = *Harboring a grudge;* unclean thoughts or desires.

A good man out of the good treasure of the heart bringeth forth good things: and an evil man out of the evil treasure bringeth forth evil things (Matthew 12:35).

For from within, out of the heart of men, proceed evil thoughts, adulteries, fornications, murders, thefts, covetousness, wickedness, deceit, lasciviousness, an evil eye, blasphemy, pride, foolishness (Mark 7:21-22).

RIFLE—See GUNS/BULLETS.

RING—*Covenant:* Authority (as in "a signet ring"); eternity (unending); prestige. **Wedding Ring** = *Covenant.*

Engagement Ring = *Promise*. **Rings Worn as Jewelry** = *Self-glorification*. (See GOLD, *Section 5*, and JEWELRY, *Section 9*.)

...The writing which is written in the king's name, and sealed with the king's ring, may no man reverse (Esther 8:8).

For if there come unto your assembly a man with a gold ring [self-glorification]*, in goodly apparel...* (James 2:2).

RIVER—*Spirit or Life (the Spirit of God, the spirit of man, or the world):* Sin; wickedness; judgment; righteousness; trial. **Deep, Wide, or Muddy River** = *Difficulty;* obstacle; impassable; incomprehensible. (See WATER, SWIMMING, and BRIDGE.)

He that believeth on Me, as the scripture hath said, out of his belly shall flow rivers of living water. (But this spake He of the Spirit, which they that believe on Him should receive...) (John 7:38-39).

Afterward he measured a thousand [mature]*; and it was a river that I could not pass over* [see Eph. 3:8]*: for the waters were risen, waters to swim in, a river that could not be passed over* (Ezekiel 47:5).

But let judgment run down as waters, and righteousness as a mighty stream (Amos 5:24).

The king's heart is in the hand of the Lord, as the rivers of water: He turneth it whithersoever He will (Proverbs 21:1).

When thou passest through the waters, I will be with thee; and through the rivers, they shall not overflow thee... (Isaiah 43:2).

DRY RIVER BED—*Barren:* Religion (as compared to true worship); tradition; backslidden condition; repented (as when Israel obeyed and crossed the Jordan on dry ground after their forefathers refused to go in and possess the land).

A drought is upon her waters [wells, lakes and rivers]; *and they shall be dried up: for it is the land of graven images, and they are mad upon their idols* (Jeremiah 50:38).

ROAD—See HIGHWAY.

ROBBERY—See THIEF, *Section 7.*

ROCKET—*Power:* Powerful ministry; swift progress; swift destruction; sudden, unexpected attack; war.

But God shall shoot at them with an arrow [or rocket]; *suddenly shall they be wounded* (Psalm 64:7).

Therefore shall his calamity come suddenly; suddenly shall he be broken without remedy (Proverbs 6:15).

He, that being often reproved hardeneth his neck, shall suddenly be destroyed, and that without remedy (Proverbs 29:1).

ROCKING CHAIR—*Old:* Past; memories; meditation; rest; retirement.

Thus saith the Lord, Stand ye in the ways, and see, and ask for [or remember] *the old paths, where is the good way, and walk therein, and ye shall find rest for your souls...* (Jeremiah 6:16).

ROLLER SKATES (or Roller Blades)—*Speed:* Fast; swift advancement or progress; skillful.

For He will finish the work, and cut it short in righteousness: because a short [quick] work will the Lord make upon the earth (Romans 9:28).

ROOF—*Covering:* Oversight; government or covenant (good or evil); Holy Spirit. **Rooftop** = *Revealed;* manifest.

Woe to the rebellious children, saith the Lord, that take counsel, but not of Me; and that cover with a covering, but not of My spirit, that they may add sin to sin (Isaiah 30:1).

What I tell you in darkness, that speak ye in light: and what ye hear in the ear, that preach ye upon the housetops (Matthew 10:27).

ROOT—*Attitude:* Hidden sin (Some common roots [wrong attitudes or values] include the following: love of money, bitterness [desire for revenge], low self-esteem, fearfulness, selfishness, an independent spirit [rebelliousness], etc.); conviction; steadfastness; pure motive; cause; reason; source; stable; unmovable.

And now also the axe is laid unto the root of the trees [God's commandment to repent] (Matthew 3:10a).

For the love of money is the root of all evil: which while some coveted after, they have erred from the faith (1 Timothy 6:10a).

Looking diligently lest any man fail of the grace of God; lest any root of bitterness springing up trouble you, and thereby many be defiled [Compare James 3:14: "But if ye have bitter envying and strife in your hearts, glory not, and lie not against the truth."] (Hebrews 12:15).

For if the firstfruit be holy, the lump is also holy: and if the root be holy, so are the branches [and fruit] (Romans 11:16).

ROPE/CORD—*Bondage:* Sin; covenant; vow; hindrances; rescue; salvation.

His own iniquities shall take the wicked himself, and he shall be holden with the cords of his sins (Proverbs 5:22).

...Bind the sacrifice with cords, even unto the horns of the altar (Psalm 118:27).

So Ebed-melech...took thence old cast clouts and old rotten rags, and let them down by cords into the dungeon to [save] *Jeremiah* (Jeremiah 38:11).

ROSE—*Romance:* Love; courtship. **Red Rose** = *Passion.* **Yellow Rose Garden** = *Marriage counseling.*

I am the rose of Sharon, and the lily of the valleys (Song of Solomon 2:1).

ROUND (Shape)—*Spiritual:* Grace; mercy; compassion; forgiveness; approximate (as in "rounding off your taxes to the nearest dollar"). (See SQUARE.)

Ye shall not round the corners of your heads, neither shalt thou mar the corners of thy beard [to round the corners is self-justification and hypocrisy, rather than judging oneself rightly] (Leviticus 19:27).

And when ye reap the harvest of your land, thou shalt not wholly reap the corners of thy field...neither shalt thou gather every grape of thy vineyard; thou shalt leave them for the poor and stranger [by rounding the corners of the fields (leaving the produce in the corners) and not completely gleaning the fields, they showed grace and mercy to the poor]... (Leviticus 19:9-10).

ROWING—*Work:* Working out life's problems (personal or ministry); earnest prayer; spiritual labor. (See BICYCLE, *Section 8.*)

And He saw them toiling in rowing; for the wind was contrary unto them (Mark 6:48a).

Because for the work of Christ he was nigh unto death, not regarding his life, to supply your lack of service toward me (Philippians 2:30).

RUB BOARD—*Rough:* Hard correction; not diplomatic; cleansing; weariness (as in "the wash woman is worn out").

The man, who is the lord of the land, spake roughly to us (Genesis 42:30a).

Wash you, make you clean; put away the evil of your doings from before Mine eyes; cease to do evil (Isaiah 1:16).

RUG—*Covering:* Covenant; Holy Spirit; deception or covering things up (as in "sweeping things under the rug").

For there is nothing hid [swept under the rug], *which shall not be manifested; neither was any thing kept secret, but that it should come abroad* (Mark 4:22).

But have renounced the hidden things of dishonesty, not walking in craftiness, nor handling the word of God deceitfully; but by manifestation of the truth commending ourselves to every man's conscience in the sight of God (2 Corinthians 4:2).

RUNNING—*Striving:* Working out one's salvation; faith; haste; trial.

Know ye not that they which run in a race run all, but one receiveth the prize? So run, that ye may obtain (1 Corinthians 9:24).

If thou hast run with the footmen, and they have wearied thee, then how canst thou contend with horses? (Jeremiah 12:5a)

RUTS—See DITCH.

SALT—*Seasoning or Preservative:* Covenant; acceptable; memorial; rejected. (See SEA.)

Salt is good: but if the salt have lost his saltiness, wherewith will ye season it? Have salt in yourselves, and have peace one with another (Mark 9:50).

Ought ye not to know that the Lord God of Israel gave the kingdom over Israel to David for ever, even to him and to his sons by a covenant of salt? (2 Chronicles 13:5)

But his wife looked back from behind him, and she became a pillar of salt (Genesis 19:26).

But the miry places thereof and the marshes thereof shall not be healed; they shall be given to salt (Ezekiel 47:11).

SAND—*Flesh:* Improper foundation; weakness; weariness; drudgery; hindrance; childish (as in a child's sandbox); unclean (as in a cat's sandbox). (See SEACOAST.)

And every one that heareth these sayings of Mine, and doeth them not, shall be likened unto a foolish man, which built his house upon the sand: and the rain descended, and the floods came, and the winds blew, and beat upon that house; and it fell: and great was the fall of it (Matthew 7:26-27).

A stone is heavy, and the sand weighty; but a fool's wrath is heavier than them both (Proverbs 27:3).

Wherefore seeing we also are compassed about with so great a cloud of witnesses, let us lay aside every weight, and the

sin which doth so easily beset us, and let us run with pa-
tience the race that is set before us (Hebrews 12:1).

SEA—*Humanity:* (*Note:* Sea [salt] water is undrinkable.)
People; nations; gentiles; barrier. **Salt Water** = *Spirit of*
the world; unclean; source of evil. **Undertow** = *Undercur-*
rent; discontent; murmuring (see Mt. 20:11).

Then thou shalt see, and flow together, and thine heart shall
fear, and be enlarged; because the abundance of the sea
[gentiles] *shall be converted unto thee, the forces of the Gen-*
tiles shall come unto thee (Isaiah 60:5).

The Lord said, I will bring again from Bashan [Heb.:
"shame" or "sleep"], *I will bring My people again from*
the depths of the sea [worldliness] (Psalm 68:22).

Doth a fountain send forth at the same place sweet water
and bitter [poison, or sea water]? *Can the fig tree, my breth-*
ren, bear olive berries? either a vine, figs? so can no fountain
both yield salt [sea] *water and fresh* (James 3:11-12).

SEACOAST—*Boundary:* Heart or soul (which contains
and limits the spirit of man); flesh; limitations; weights.
(See SAND.)

Fear ye not Me? saith the Lord: will ye not tremble at My
presence, which have placed the sand [seed of Abraham,
i.e., the Church] *for the bound of the sea* [people of the
world (see SEA)] *by a perpetual decree, that it cannot pass*
it (Jeremiah 5:22a).

O thou sword of the Lord, how long will it be ere thou be
quiet? put up thyself into thy scabbard, rest, and be still.
How can it be quiet, seeing the Lord hath given it a charge
against Ashkelon [Heb.: "the fire of infamy," i.e., evil

passion], *and against the sea shore* [flesh]? *there hath He appointed it* (Jeremiah 47:6-7).

SEED—*Word:* Word of God; saints; faith; word of man (revealing the heart); Christ; fullness of iniquity (as in "weeds gone to seed"). (See WEEDS.)

Now the parable is this: The seed is the word of God (Luke 8:11).

The field is the world; the good seed are the children of the kingdom; but the tares are the children of the wicked one (Matthew 13:38).

And the Lord said, If ye had faith as a grain of mustard seed, ye might say unto this sycamine tree, Be thou plucked up by the root, and be thou planted in the sea; and it should obey you (Luke 17:6).

A good man out of the good treasure of his heart bringeth forth that which is good; and an evil man out of the evil treasure of his heart bringeth forth that which is evil: for of the abundance of the heart his mouth speaketh [produces good or bad seed, revealing his heart] (Luke 6:45).

SELF-RISING FLOUR—See LEAVEN.

SEWAGE—*Corruption:* Filthiness of the flesh; sin; evil; corrupt authority; abuse of authority.

When the Lord shall have washed away the filth of the daughters of Zion...by the spirit of judgment, and by the spirit of burning (Isaiah 4:4).

And thou shalt have a paddle upon thy weapon; and it shall be, when thou wilt ease thyself abroad, thou shalt dig therewith, and shalt turn back [remember and acknowledge] *and cover* [confess your sins] *that which cometh from thee: for the Lord thy God walketh in the midst of thy camp, to deliver thee, and to give up thine enemies before thee; therefore shall thy camp be holy: that He see no unclean thing in thee, and turn away from thee* (Deuteronomy 23:13-14).

For he that soweth to his flesh shall of the flesh reap corruption... (Galatians 6:8).

SEWING—*Joining:* Union; reunion; counseling; reconciliation. **Sewing Notions** = *Inclination* (as in "I've got a notion to join the army"); idea.

And it came to pass...that the soul of Jonathan was knit [tied or sewed] *with the soul of David, and Jonathan loved him as his own soul* (1 Samuel 18:1).

SEX—*Agreement:* Covenant; unity; taken advantage of, or "used"; abuse of authority; when naturally interpreted it means love or fornication. **Masturbation** = *Self-gratification;* inordinate self-love; selfishness. **Genitals** = *Secret;* private matter; shame. (Concerning sex outside of marriage, see HOMOSEXUAL ACTS, KISS, HARLOT, *Section 7,* ADULTERY, BESTIALITY, and RAPE; also see Chapter Two of this book: "Interpreting Your Dreams," subheading, "R- and X-Rated Dreams"; for sex in marriage, see MARRIAGE).

Know ye not that your bodies are the members of Christ? shall I then take the members of Christ, and make them the members of an harlot? God forbid. What? know ye not that he which is joined to an harlot is one body? for two, saith he, shall be one flesh (1 Corinthians 6:15-16).

But if they cannot contain, let them marry: for it is better to marry than to burn [with lust] (1 Corinthians 7:9).

And if a man entice a maid that is not betrothed, and lie with her, he shall surely endow her to be his wife (Exodus 22:16).

Will ye steal, murder, and commit adultery, and swear falsely, and burn incense unto Baal, and walk after other gods whom ye know not; and come and stand before Me in this house, which is called by My name, and say, We are delivered to do all these abominations? (Jeremiah 7:9-10)

Therefore the Lord will smite with a scab the crown of the head of the daughters of Zion, and the Lord will discover [reveal] *their secret parts* [genitals, i.e., hidden sin] (Isaiah 3:17).

SHAVING—See HAIR.

SHIRT—See COAT.

SHOES/BOOTS—*Words:* Gospel; covenant; preparation. **New Shoes** = *New ministry or way of life.* **House Slippers** = *Self-examination.* **Loafers** = *Casual;* at ease; unconcern; hypocrisy; loafing. **Combat or Heavy Boots** = *Spiritual warfare.* **Steel-Towed Boots** = *Protection.* (See FEET.)

And your feet shod with the preparation of the gospel of peace (Ephesians 6:15).

Now this was the manner in former time in Israel concerning redeeming and concerning changing, for to confirm all things; a man plucked off his shoe, and gave it to his neighbor [as we would say, "I give you my word."]: *and this was a testimony in Israel* (Ruth 4:7).

This I say then, Walk in the Spirit, and ye shall not fulfil the lust of the flesh (Galatians 5:16).

SHOULDER—*Support:* Bearer (as in "burden bearer"); government; authority; responsibility; stubborn (see NECK). **Broad Shoulders** = *Strength;* consolation. **Drooped Shoulders** = *Tired;* overburdened; discouraged; hopelessness. **Bare Female Shoulders** = *Seduction;* temptation; witchcraft.

> *I removed his shoulder from the burden: his hands were delivered from the pots* (Psalm 81:6).

> *For unto us a child is born, unto us a son is given: and the government shall be upon His shoulder...* (Isaiah 9:6).

> *But they refused to hearken, and pulled away the shoulder, and stopped their ears, that they should not hear* (Zechariah 7:11).

SHOVEL—*Tongue:* Prayer; confession; gossip; slander; dig; search; inquire.

> *And he said, Thus saith the Lord, Make this valley full of ditches* [pray]. *For thus saith the Lord, Ye shall not see wind, neither shall ye see rain; yet that valley shall be filled with water* (2 Kings 3:16-17a).

> *And thou shalt have a paddle* [shovel blade] *upon thy weapon; and it shall be, when thou wilt ease thyself abroad, thou shalt dig therewith* [confess], *and shalt turn back* [repent] *and cover that* [uncleanness of the flesh, i.e., sin] *which cometh from thee* (Deuteronomy 23:13).

> *An ungodly man diggeth up evil: and in his lips there is as a burning fire* (Proverbs 16:27).

> *Whoso diggeth a pit* [with words or deeds] *shall fall therein: and he that rolleth a stone, it will return upon him* (Proverbs 26:27).

SHOWER—See BATHING.

SIDEWALK—See PATH.

SIGN—*Directions:* **Stop Sign** = *Stop.* **Yield** = *Yield.* **Detour** = *Change of direction.* **Intersection** = *Decision or change.* **Keep off the Grass** = *Give no man offense.*

I have also spoken by the prophets, and I have multiplied visions, and used similitudes [visible signs], *by the ministry of the prophets* (Hosea 12:10).

Give none offence, neither to the Jews, nor to the Gentiles, nor to the church of God [Compare First Peter 1:24a: "For all flesh is as grass."] (1 Corinthians 10:32).

SKATEBOARD—*Balance:* Skillful maneuvering; skillful ministry; risky; fast. (See ROLLER SKATES.)

As for these four children, God gave them knowledge and skill in all learning and wisdom: and Daniel had understanding in all visions and dreams (Daniel 1:17).

SKIING (Water or Snow Skiing)—*Faith:* Supported by God's power through faith; fast progress.

So when they had rowed about five and twenty or thirty furlongs, they see Jesus walking on the sea, and drawing nigh unto the ship: and they were afraid. ... Then they willingly received Him into the ship: and immediately the ship was at the land whither they went (John 6:19,21).

And He said, Come. And when Peter was come down out of the ship, he walked on the water, to go to Jesus. But when he saw the wind boisterous, he [lost his faith and] *was afraid; and beginning to sink, he cried, saying, Lord, save me. And immediately Jesus stretched forth His hand, and caught him, and said unto him, O thou of little faith, wherefore didst thou doubt?* (Matthew 14:29-31)

SKIRT—*Covering:* Grace. **Lack of a Skirt** = *Uncovered;* shame because of sin; hypocrisy. (See CLOTHING.)

Also in thy skirts [that which is covered, or hidden] *is found the blood of the souls of the poor innocents: I have not found it by secret search, but upon all these* (Jeremiah 2:34).

Therefore will I discover thy skirts upon thy face [as when the wind blows a woman's skirt over her head], *that thy shame may appear* [be revealed] (Jeremiah 13:26).

SLEEP—*Unconscious:* Unaware (hidden or covered); ignorant; danger; death; rest; laziness. **Oversleep** = *Late;* to miss an appointment.

For the Lord hath poured out upon you the spirit of deep sleep, and hath closed your eyes: the prophets and your rulers, the seers hath He covered (Isaiah 29:10).

And that, knowing the time, that now it is high time to awake out of sleep: for now is our salvation nearer than when we believed (Romans 13:11).

It is vain for you to rise up early, to sit up late, to eat the bread of sorrows: for so He giveth His beloved sleep (Psalm 127:2).

Love not sleep, lest thou come to poverty; open thine eyes, and thou shalt be satisfied with bread (Proverbs 20:13).

SMILE—*Friendly:* Kindness; benevolent; good will; without offense; seduction. (See KISS, LIPS, and TEETH.)

A man that hath friends must show himself friendly [smile]: *and there is a friend that sticketh closer than a brother* (Proverbs 18:24).

SMOKE—*Manifest Presence:* Evidence (as in "where there's smoke, there's fire"); to manifest (as smoke manifests a fire); glory of God; prayer; lying or boasting (as in "blowing smoke"); offense; temporary; cover-up (as in "a smoke screen"). (See SMOKING.)

> *And one cried unto another, and said, Holy, holy, holy, is the Lord of hosts: the whole earth is full of His glory...and the house was filled with smoke* (Isaiah 6:3-4).

> *And the smoke of the incense, which came with the prayers of the saints, ascended up before God out of the angel's hand* (Revelation 8:4).

> *And when he looked on him, he was afraid, and said, What is it, Lord? And he said unto him, Thy prayers and thine alms are come up* [as incense] *for a memorial before God* (Acts 10:4).

> *As vinegar to the teeth, and as smoke to the eyes, so is the sluggard to them that send him* (Proverbs 10:26).

> *And he looked toward Sodom and Gomorrah...and, lo, the smoke of the country went up as the smoke of a furnace* [God's judgment manifest] (Genesis 19:28).

SMOKING—*Pride:* **Smoking Cigarettes** = *Pride or bitterness;* bitter memories; offense; unforgiving; envy; jealousy; self-righteousness. **Smoking a Cigar** = *Haughty;* arrogant. **Smoking a Pipe** = *Intellectual pride.* **Smoking Furnace** = *Offense;* anger; trouble.

> *Which say, Stand by thyself, come not near to me; for I am holier than thou. These are a smoke in my nose* [as another person's cigarette smoke offends a non-smoker], *a fire that burneth all the day* (Isaiah 65:5).

Proud and haughty scorner is his name, who dealeth in proud wrath (Proverbs 21:24).

...We know that we all have knowledge. Knowledge puffeth up, but charity edifieth (1 Corinthians 8:1).

And it come to pass, when he heareth the words of this curse, that he bless [justify, or approve of] *himself in his heart, saying, I shall have peace, though I walk in the imagination of mine heart, to add drunkenness to thirst: the Lord will not spare him, but then the anger of the Lord and His jealousy shall smoke against that man...* (Deuteronomy 29:19-20).

SNOW/ICE—*Word:* **Snow** = *Pure;* grace; covered; unrevealed; unfulfilled. **Dirty Snow** = *Impure.* **Snowdrift** = *Barrier;* hindrance; opposition; snare. **Ice** = *Hard Saying;* slippery; dangerous (as in "skating on thin ice"). (See HAIL.)

For as the rain cometh down, and the snow from heaven, and returneth not thither, but watereth the earth, and maketh it bring forth and bud, that it may give seed to the sower, and bread to the eater: so shall My word be that goeth forth out of My mouth (Isaiah 55:10-11a).

Shall vain words have an end? or what emboldeneth thee that thou answerest? I also could speak as ye do: if your soul were in my soul's stead, I could heap up words against you [as a snowdrift] (Job 16:3-4a).

Many therefore of His disciples, when they had heard this, said, This is an hard saying; who can hear it? (John 6:60)

But as for me, my feet were almost gone; my steps had well nigh slipped (Psalm 73:2).

SNOWSHOES—*Faith:* Walking in the Spirit; supported by faith in the Word of God. (**Snow** = *Word.* **Snowshoes** = *Faith.*) (See SNOW and SKIING.)

> ...*When Peter was come down out of the ship, he walked on the water, to go to Jesus* (Matthew 14:29).

> *For we walk by faith, not by sight* (2 Corinthians 5:7).

SOAP—*Cleansing:* Conviction; forgiveness; prayer; repentance.

> *For though thou wash thee with nitre* [strong soap], *and take thee much soap, yet thine iniquity is marked before Me, saith the Lord God* (Jeremiah 2:22).

> *Wash you, make you clean; put away the evil of your doings from before Mine eyes; cease to do evil* (Isaiah 1:16).

SOCKS—*Covering (same as an undergarment):* **Socks Without Shoes** = *Without full preparation.* **White Socks** = *Pure heart.* **Black or Dirty Socks** = *Impure heart.* (See WHITE, BLACK, *Section 3.* See also FEET, SHOES, *Section 9.*)

> *And your feet shod with the preparation of the gospel of peace* [both word (shoes) and spirit (socks)] (Ephesians 6:15).

> *This I say then, Walk in the Spirit* [white socks], *and ye shall not fulfil the lust of the flesh* (Galatians 5:16).

> *He that hath clean hands, and a pure heart* [white socks]; *who hath not lifted up his soul unto vanity, nor sworn deceitfully* [black or dirty socks] (Psalm 24:4).

SPRING—*(New) Beginning:* Revival; fresh start; renewal; regeneration; salvation; refreshing.

For, lo, the winter is past, the rain is over and gone; the flowers appear on the earth; the time of the singing of birds is come, and the voice of the turtle is heard in our land (Song of Solomon 2:11-12).

Behold, I will do a new thing; now it shall spring forth; shall ye not know it? I will even make a way in the wilderness, and rivers in the desert (Isaiah 43:19).

Repent ye therefore, and be converted, that your sins may be blotted out, when the times of refreshing shall come from the presence of the Lord (Acts 3:19).

SQUARE (Shape)—*Legalistic:* Religious or religion (speaking the truth without love); no mercy; hard or harsh; of the world. (See ROUND.)

And when ye reap the harvest of your land, thou shalt not wholly reap the corners of thy field [making them square], *neither shalt thou gather the gleanings of thy harvest* [thus showing mercy to the needy] (Leviticus 19:9).

STAIRS—*Steps (as in a process, sometimes including the concept of time):* Promotion; ambition (self-promotion); procedure. **Stairs Going Down** = *Demotion;* backslide; failure. **Guardrail** = *Safety;* precaution; warning to be careful. (See LADDER.)

Neither shalt thou go up by steps unto Mine altar [self-promotion or politics], *that thy nakedness be not discovered thereon* (Exodus 20:26).

Then they hasted, and took every man his garment, and put it under him on the top of the stairs, and blew with trumpets, saying, Jehu is king (2 Kings 9:13).

When thou buildest a new house, then thou shalt make a battlement [wall or guardrail] *for thy roof* [or stairway], *that thou bring not blood upon thine house, if any man fall from thence* (Deuteronomy 22:8).

STAR—*Person:* Christian; apostle; saint; preacher; minister; leader or role model (good and bad, as a hero or movie star).

That in blessing I will bless thee, and in multiplying I will multiply thy seed as the stars of the heaven...and thy seed shall possess the gate of his enemies (Genesis 22:17).

And he [Joseph] dreamed yet another dream, and told it his brethren, and said, Behold...the sun and the moon and the eleven stars made obeisance to me...and his father rebuked him, and said unto him...Shall I and thy mother and thy brethren indeed come to bow down ourselves to thee to the earth? (Genesis 37:9-10)

And they that be wise shall shine as the brightness of the firmament; and they that turn many to righteousness as the stars for ever and ever (Daniel 12:3).

And his tail [the false prophet (see Is. 9:15)] *drew the third part of the stars of heaven* [Christians (see Dan. 11:33-35)], *and did cast them to the earth: and the dragon stood before the woman which was ready to be delivered, for to devour her child as soon as it was born* (Revelation 12:4).

Raging waves of the sea, foaming out their own shame; wandering stars, to whom is reserved the blackness of darkness for ever (Jude 1:13).

STEPS—See STAIRS.

STONE—*Witness:* Word; testimony; person; precept; accusations; persecution (as in false witness).

And Joshua said unto all the people, Behold, this stone shall be a witness unto us; for it hath heard all the words of the Lord which He spake unto us (Joshua 24:27a).

A man also or woman that hath a familiar spirit, or that is a wizard, shall surely be put to death: they shall stone them with stones [public witness or accusation]... (Leviticus 20:27).

Ye also, as lively stones [witnesses (see Acts 1:8)], *are built up a spiritual house* (1 Peter 2:5a).

STORM—*Disturbance:* Change; spiritual warfare; judgment; sudden calamity or destruction; trial; persecution; opposition; witchcraft. **White Storm** = *God's power;* revival. (See CLOUDS, THUNDER, and WIND.)

For Thou hast been a strength to the poor, a strength to the needy in his distress, a refuge from the storm, a shadow from the heat, when the blast of the terrible ones is as a storm against the wall [an attack against the defenses of the righteousness] (Isaiah 25:4).

For when they shall say, Peace and safety; then sudden destruction cometh upon them, as travail upon a woman with child; and they shall not escape (1 Thessalonians 5:3).

The Lord hath His way in the whirlwind and in the storm, and the clouds are the dust of His feet (Nahum 1:3b).

STOVE—See FURNACE and OVEN.

STREET—See HIGHWAY.

STUMBLE—*Fail:* Sin; backslide; mistake; become deceived; to be overcome; obstacle; ignorance.

But if a man walk in the night, he stumbleth [sins], *because there is no light in him* (John 11:10).

The bows of the mighty men are broken, and they that stumbled [failed through weakness] *are girded with strength* (1 Samuel 2:4).

When the wicked, even mine enemies and my foes, came upon me to eat up my flesh, they stumbled and fell [into their own snare] (Psalm 27:2).

STUMP—See TREE STUMP.

SUGAR—See HONEY.

SUICIDE—*Self-Destruction:* Self-hatred; grief; remorse; foolish action.

Be not righteous over much; neither make thyself over wise: why shouldest thou destroy thyself? (Ecclesiastes 7:16)

And he [Judas] *cast down the pieces of silver in the temple* [in remorse], *and departed, and went and hanged himself* (Matthew 27:5).

SUITCASE—*Personal:* Heart; travel; move; temporary (as in "living out of a suitcase").

Therefore, thou son of man, prepare thee stuff for removing [i.e., pack your bags], *and remove by day in their sight; and thou shalt remove from thy place to another place* (Ezekiel 12:3a).

For every man shall bear his own burden [personal responsibility] (Galatians 6:5).

SUMMER—*Harvest:* Harvest time; opportunity (as in "make hay while the sun shines"); trial; heat of affliction. (See SUN.)

For day and night Thy hand was heavy upon me: my moisture is turned into the drought of summer... (Psalm 32:4).

He that gathereth in summer is a wise son: but he that sleepeth in harvest is a son that causeth shame (Proverbs 10:5).

SUN—*Heat:* God; light; goodness; affliction; persecution; trial; god of this world (arousing the heat of passion).

For the Lord God is a sun and shield (Psalm 84:11a).

But unto you that fear My name shall the Sun of righteousness arise with healing in His wings (Malachi 4:2a).

But when the sun was up, it was scorched; and because it had no root, it withered away. ... And have no root in themselves, and so endure but for a time: afterward, when affliction or persecution ariseth for the word's sake, immediately they are offended (Mark 4:6,17).

SWEEPING—*Cleaning:* Repentance; change (as in "a sweeping change"); removing obstacles; rebuking evil doers. (See BROOM.)

Judgment also will I lay to the line, and righteousness to the plummet: and the hail shall sweep away the refuge of lies... (Isaiah 28:17).

Let all bitterness, and wrath, and anger, and clamor, and evil speaking, be put away from you, with all malice (Ephesians 4:31).

Having therefore these promises, dearly beloved, let us cleanse ourselves from all filthiness of the flesh and spirit, perfecting holiness in the fear of God (2 Corinthians 7:1).

For behold this selfsame thing, that ye sorrowed after a godly sort [repented], *what carefulness it wrought in you, yea, what clearing of yourselves, yea, what indignation, yea, what fear, yea, what vehement desire, yea, what zeal, yea, what revenge! In all things ye have approved yourselves to be clear* [or clean] *in this matter* (2 Corinthians 7:11).

Them that sin rebuke before all, that others also may fear (1 Timothy 5:20).

SWIMMING—*Spiritual (as in spiritual acts or activity):* Serving God; worshiping; operating in the gifts of the Spirit; prophesying. (See RIVER, WATER, and DROWN.)

Afterward he measured a thousand; and it was a river [of God's Spirit] *that I could not pass over: for the waters were risen, waters to swim in, a river that could not be passed over* (Ezekiel 47:5).

Unto me, who am less than the least of all saints, is this grace given, that I should preach among the Gentiles the unsearchable riches [the deep things of God which cannot be passed over] *of Christ* (Ephesians 3:8).

SWIMMING POOL—*Spiritual Place or Condition:* Church; home; family; God's blessings. **Dirty or Dry Pool or Pond** = *Corrupt or destitute spiritual condition;* backslidden.

I will open rivers in high places, and fountains in the midst of the valleys: I will make the wilderness a pool of water, and the dry land springs of water (Isaiah 41:18).

A drought is upon her waters [swimming pools, lakes, and rivers]*; and they shall be dried up: for it is the land of graven images, and they are mad upon their idols* (Jeremiah 50:38).

As for thee also, by the blood of thy covenant I have sent forth thy prisoners out of the pit wherein is no water (Zechariah 9:11).

SWING (PORCH)—*Peaceful:* Rest; quietness; romance; fellowship. **Swinging High (Park Swing)** = *Danger;* immorality; infidelity.

...In returning and rest shall ye be saved; in quietness and in confidence shall be your strength... (Isaiah 30:15).

SWORD—*Words:* Word of God; critical words; evil intent; threat; strife; war; persecution. (See KNIVES.)

And take the helmet of salvation, and the sword of the Spirit, which is the word of God (Ephesians 6:17).

Who whet [sharpen] *their tongue like a sword, and bend their bows to shoot their arrows, even bitter words* (Psalm 64:3).

There is that speaketh like the piercings of a sword: but the tongue of the wise is health (Proverbs 12:18).

And there went out another horse that was red: and power [authority] *was given to him that sat thereon to take peace from the earth, and that they should kill one another: and there was given unto him a great sword* [of persecution] (Revelation 6:4).

TABLE—*Communion:* Agreement; covenant; conference; provision. **Under the Table** = *Deceitful dealings;* hidden motives; evil intent.

But I say, that the things which the Gentiles sacrifice, they sacrifice to devils, and not to God: and I would not that ye should have fellowship [communion] *with devils. Ye cannot drink the cup of the Lord, and the cup of devils: ye cannot be partakers of the Lord's table, and of the table of devils* (1 Corinthians 10:20-21).

And both these kings' hearts shall be to do mischief, and they shall speak lies at one [conference] *table; but it shall not prosper...* (Daniel 11:27).

Yea, they spake against God; they said, Can God furnish a table in the wilderness? (Psalm 78:19)

TAIL—*Last in Time, Rank, or Importance:* That which follows; afterward; least. **Wagging Tail** = *Friendly*. **Tucked Tail** = *Guilt;* shame; cowardly. (See DOG, *Section 1.*)

The ancient and honorable, he is the head; and the prophet that teacheth lies, he is the tail (Isaiah 9:15).

And the Lord shall make thee the head, and not the tail; and thou shalt be above only, and thou shalt not be beneath... (Deuteronomy 28:13).

He shall lend to thee, and thou shalt not lend to him: he shall be the head, and thou shalt be the tail (Deuteronomy 28:44).

TAR—*Covering:* Repair; patch; bitterness; offense; hatred; grudge.

And when she could not longer hide him [Moses], *she took for him an ark of bulrushes, and daubed it with slime and with pitch* [tar], *and put the child therein; and she laid it in the flags by the river's brink* (Exodus 2:3).

For it is the day of the Lord's vengeance, and the year of recompenses for the controversy of Zion. And the streams thereof shall be turned into pitch [tar]...*and the land thereof shall become burning pitch* (Isaiah 34:8-9).

TASTING—*Experience:* Discern; try; test; judge. (See TEETH and CHEWING.)

...Cannot my taste discern perverse things? (Job 6:30)

O taste and see that the Lord is good (Psalm 34:8a).

But we see Jesus, who was made...for the suffering of death...that He by the grace of God should taste [experience] *death for every man* (Hebrews 2:9).

TEA (also Ice Tea)—*Refreshing:* Grace; good news; salvation; time of refreshing; (as in "tea time"); revival.

As cold waters [or ice tea] *to a thirsty soul, so is good news* [the gospel] *from a far country* [Heaven] (Proverbs 25:25).

To whom He said, This is the rest wherewith ye may cause the weary to rest; and this is the refreshing: yet they would not hear (Isaiah 28:12).

Repent ye therefore, and be converted, that your sins may be blotted out, when the times of refreshing shall come from the presence of the Lord (Acts 3:19).

TEARS—*Grief:* Sorrow; anguish; repentance; prayer; judgment.

And straightway the father of the child cried out, and said with tears [heartfelt repentance], *Lord, I believe; help Thou mine unbelief* (Mark 9:24).

This poor man cried, and the Lord heard him, and saved him out of all his troubles (Psalm 34:6).

TEETH—*Wisdom (especially wisdom teeth):* Experience; work out (as in "work out your own salvation"). **Brushing Teeth** = *Cleaning one's thoughts or words;* meditation. **Animal Teeth (Lion's, Wolf's, etc.)** = *Danger.* (See FOOD/MILK, CHEWING. See also WOLF, *Section 1.*)

For when for the time ye ought to be teachers, ye have need that one teach you again which be the first principles of the oracles of God; and are become such as have need of milk, and not of strong meat. For every one that useth milk is un-skillful in the word of righteousness: for he is a babe [has baby teeth]. *But strong meat belongeth to them that are of full age* [with adult teeth], *even those who by reason of use have their senses exercised to discern both good and evil* [wisdom] (Hebrews 5:12-14).

And I will take away his blood out of his mouth, and his abominations from between his teeth...and no oppressor shall pass through them any more... (Zechariah 9:7-8).

Wherewithal shall a young man cleanse his way? by taking heed thereto according to Thy word (Psalm 119:9).

BABY TEETH—*Immaturity:* Without experience; without wisdom or knowledge; innocent.

For before the child shall know to refuse the evil, and choose the good [replace baby teeth with adult teeth], *the land that thou abhorrest shall be forsaken of both her kings* [See Hebrews 5:12-14.] (Isaiah 7:16).

FALSE TEETH—*False or Replacement:* Wisdom or knowledge gained through experience or previous failures; logical reasoning (e.g., philosophy replacing truth); tradition; error.

And not only so, but we glory in tribulations [working out our salvation] *also: knowing that tribulation worketh patience; and patience, experience* [thus ignorance is replaced by wisdom]; *and experience, hope* (Romans 5:3-4).

Beware lest any man spoil you [replace the truth] *through* [or with] *philosophy and vain deceit, after the tradition of men, after the rudiments of the world, and not after Christ* (Colossians 2:8).

O Timothy, keep that which is committed to thy trust, avoiding profane and vain babblings, and oppositions of science falsely so called [replacing truth with the falsehoods of deceived, "learned" men] (1 Timothy 6:20).

TOOTHACHE—*Trial:* Trouble. **Broken Tooth** = *Bad experience;* problem; gaining wisdom (learning obedience) through suffering (Tooth = *Wisdom;* ache = *Suffering*). **Broken** = *Potential pain* (when or if pressure is applied); unfaithful; undependable friend or person; no faith; unbelief.

[Unwise] *Confidence in an unfaithful man in time of trouble is like a broken tooth, and a foot out of joint* (Proverbs 25:19).

Though He were a Son, yet learned He obedience by the things which He suffered (Hebrews 5:8).

What mean ye, that ye use this proverb concerning the land of Israel, saying, The fathers have eaten sour grapes, and the children's teeth are set on edge? (Ezekiel 18:2)

TELEPHONE—*Communication:* Prayer; message from God; counsel; gossip; enemy's voice. **Phone Inoperative or Busy** = *Prayer hindered.*

...Whosoever shall call on the name of the Lord shall be saved (Acts 2:21).

...The same Lord over all is rich unto all that call upon Him (Romans 10:12).

Behold, the Lord's hand is not shortened, that it cannot save; neither His ear heavy, that it cannot hear: but...your sins have hid His face from you, that He will not hear (Isaiah 59:1-2).

Regard not them that have familiar spirits, neither seek [call upon or enquire] *after wizards, to be defiled by them...* (Leviticus 19:31).

TELESCOPE—*Future:* Prophetic vision of the future; at a distance; far away in time. (See BINOCULARS.)

After this I looked, and, behold, a door was opened in heaven: and the first voice...said, Come up hither, and I will show thee things which must be hereafter (Revelation 4:1).

TELEVISION—*Vision:* Message; prophecy; preaching; news; evil influence; wickedness.

He hath said, which heard the words of God, and knew the knowledge of the most High, which saw the vision of the Almighty, falling into a trance, but having his eyes open (Numbers 24:16).

Then was the secret revealed unto Daniel in a night vision (Daniel 2:19a).

And they carried the ark [gospel] *of God in a new cart* [television evangelism] *out of the house of Abinadab* [Heb.: "father of generosity," i.e., liberal giving]*: and Uzza* [Heb.: "strength of man," i.e., money] *and Ahio* [Heb.: "brotherly," i.e., agreement of man] *drave the cart. ... And when they came unto the threshingfloor of Chidon, Uzza put forth his hand to hold the ark; for the oxen* [ministers] *stumbled* [sinned]. *And the anger of the Lord was kindled against Uzza* [commerce, money, the source of man's strength], *and He smote him* [bringing economic depression], *because he put his hand to the ark: and there he died before God* (1 Chronicles 13:7, 9-10).

Who knowing the judgment of God, that they which commit such things are worthy of death, not only do the same, but have pleasure in [watching] *them that do them* (Romans 1:32).

THIGH—*Flesh:* The natural man; works of the flesh; lust; seduction. (See LEGS.)

And as he passed over Penuel the sun rose upon him, and he halted upon his thigh [i.e., the power of the flesh was broken as a result of his encounter with God]. *Therefore the children of Israel eat not of the sinew which shrank, which is upon the hollow of the thigh, unto this day* [we are not to partake of the life of the flesh]... (Genesis 32:31-32).

Then the priest shall charge the woman with an oath of cursing...The Lord make thee a curse and an oath among thy people, when the Lord doth make thy thigh [flesh] *to rot* [i.e., sickness], *and thy belly* [spirit] *to swell* [i.e., puffed up in pride, haughty, angry, etc.] (Numbers 5:21).

...Uncover thy locks, make bare the leg, uncover the thigh [reveal the hidden works of the flesh]... (Isaiah 47:2).

THORNS—*Hindrance:* Gossip; evil circumstance; persecution; cares of this life; curse; defense (as in "a hedge of thorns"). **Stickers or Cockleburs** = *Irritant;* irritated (as in "a burr under his saddle"); minor afflictions.

But that which beareth thorns and briers is rejected, and is nigh unto cursing; whose end is to be burned (Hebrews 6:8).

If fire break out [rumor or gossip], *and catch in thorns* [becomes a curse to the one slandered], *so that the stacks of corn, or the standing corn, or the field, be consumed therewith; he that kindled the fire shall surely make restitution* (Exodus 22:6).

He also that received seed among the thorns is he that heareth the word; and the care of this world, and the deceitfulness of riches [and pleasures of this life (see Lk. 8:14)], *choke the word, and he becometh unfruitful* (Matthew 13:22).

THUNDER—*Change or Without Understanding (of what the Spirit is saying or of the signs of the times):* Dispensational change (i.e., a change in the way God deals with His people); a warning of impending judgment or trouble. (See STORM and TRUMPET.)

[Jesus said] *Father, glorify Thy name. Then came there a voice from heaven, saying, I have both glorified it, and will glorify it again. The people therefore, that stood by, and heard it, said that it thundered: others said, An angel spake to Him* (John 12:28-29).

The Lord also thundered in the heavens, and the Highest gave His voice; hail stones and coals of fire (Psalm 18:13).

TITLE/DEED—*Ownership:* Authorization; possession.

And the field, and the cave that is therein, were made sure [deeded] *unto Abraham for a possession of a buryingplace by the sons of Heth* (Genesis 23:20).

TNT—See DYNAMITE.

TONGUE—See BOW/ARROWS, PEN/PENCIL, and SHOVEL.

TREE(S)—*Person or Covering:* Leader; shelter; false worship; evil influence. **Oak Tree** = *Strong shelter.* **Willow Tree** = *Sorrow.* **Evergreen Tree** = *Eternal life.* (See GREEN; for **Christmas Tree**, see CHRISTMAS.)

I have seen the wicked in great power, and spreading himself like a green bay tree (Psalm 37:35).

But I am like a green olive tree in the house of God... (Psalm 52:8).

The righteous shall flourish like the palm tree: he shall grow like a cedar [evergreen] *in Lebanon* (Psalm 92:12).

And they set them up images and groves in every high hill, and under every green tree (2 Kings 17:10).

By the rivers of Babylon, there we sat down, yea, we wept, when we remembered Zion. We hanged our harps upon the willows in the midst thereof (Psalm 137:1-2).

And all the trees [people] *of the field* [world] *shall know that I the Lord have brought down the high tree* [haughty person]*, have exalted the low tree* [humble person]*, have dried up the green tree* [carnal person]*, and have made the dry tree* [repented person, dead with Christ] *to flourish* [prosper]*...* (Ezekiel 17:24).

TREE STUMP—*Stubborn:* Unbelief; roots; tenacious; obstacle; unmovable; hope or promise of restoration; regeneration.

For there is hope of a tree, if it be cut down, that it will sprout again, and that the tender branch thereof will not cease. Though the root thereof wax old in the earth, and the stock thereof die in the ground; yet through the scent of water it will bud, and bring forth boughs like a plant (Job 14:7-9).

TRIP—See STUMBLE.

TROPHY—*Memorial:* Evidence of victory; award; competition; victory in spiritual warfare.

> *And the king of Israel answered and said, Tell him, Let not him that girdeth on his harness* [sword] *boast himself as he that putteth it off* [as though he already had the victor's cup] (1 Kings 20:11).

> *And as David returned from the slaughter of the Philistine, Abner took him, and brought him before Saul with the head of the Philistine in his hand* (1 Samuel 17:57).

TRUMPET—*Voice:* Announcement; preaching; prophesying; warning; call to assemble; worship; tongues; the Rapture. **Sounding Reveille** = *Beginning;* wake up; call to assemble. **Playing Taps** = *End;* finished.

> *Cry aloud, spare not, lift up thy voice like a trumpet* [preach and prophesy], *and show My people their transgression, and the house of Jacob their sins* (Isaiah 58:1).

> *For if the* [voice of the] *trumpet give an uncertain sound* [a message in tongues without interpretation], *who shall prepare himself to the battle?* (1 Corinthians 14:8)

> *In a moment, in the twinkling of an eye, at the last trump: for the trumpet shall sound, and the dead shall be raised incorruptible, and we shall be changed* (1 Corinthians 15:52).

> *Blow the trumpet in Zion, sanctify a fast, call a solemn assembly* (Joel 2:15).

> *Wherefore he saith, Awake thou that sleepest, and arise from the dead, and Christ shall give thee light* (Ephesians 5:14).

TUNNEL—*Passage:* Transition; way of escape; troubling experience; trial; hope (as in "light at the end of the tunnel").

There hath no temptation taken you but such as is common to man: but God is faithful, who will not suffer you to be tempted above that ye are able; but will with the temptation also make a way to escape, that ye may be able to bear it (1 Corinthians 10:13).

UNDERTOW—See SEA.

URINATING—*Spirit:* **Full Bladder** = *Pressure;* compelling urge; temptation (as in sexual lust or strife). **Bladder Infection or Cancer** = *Offense;* enmity.

The beginning of strife is as when one letteth out water: therefore leave off contention [or lust], *before it be meddled with* (Proverbs 17:14).

So and more also do God unto the enemies of David, if I leave of all that pertain to him by the morning light any that pisseth against the wall (1 Samuel 25:22).

VACUUM CLEANER—See BROOM.

VAIL or VEIL—*Concealment:* Hidden; concealed (or revealed if vail or curtains are removed); covering; deception; without understanding; law; flesh.

Then opened He [the vail or curtains of] *their understanding, that they might understand the scriptures* (Luke 24:45).

And not as Moses, which put a veil over his face, that the children of Israel could not stedfastly look to the end of that which is abolished: but their minds were blinded: for until this day remaineth the same veil untaken away in the reading of the old testament; which veil is done away in Christ [see Mk. 15:37-38]. *But even unto this day, when Moses is read, the veil is upon their heart. Nevertheless when it* [the nation of Israel] *shall turn to the Lord, the veil* [conceal-ment] *shall be taken away* (2 Corinthians 3:13-16).

And Jesus cried with a loud voice, and gave up the ghost [His flesh or "veil" having been pierced (torn)]. *And the veil of the temple was rent in twain from the top to the bottom* (Mark 15:37-38).

VEGETABLES—See GARDEN.

VINE—*Source or People:* Christ; person; family; city; nation; flesh; entanglement; snare.

I [Christ] *am the vine* [source], *ye are the branches: He that abideth in Me, and I in him, the same bringeth forth much fruit...* (John 15:5).

Yet I had planted thee a noble vine [nation or people], *wholly a right seed: how then art thou turned into the degenerate plant of a strange vine unto Me?* (Jeremiah 2:21)

And the vine said unto them, Should I leave my wine, which cheereth God and man, and go to be promoted over the trees? (Judges 9:13)

VOLCANO—*Eruption:* Sudden violent reaction to pressure; emotionally unstable (as in sudden anger); trouble erupting; God's judgment.

For a fire is kindled in Mine anger, and shall burn unto the lowest hell, and shall consume the earth with her increase, and set on fire the foundations of the mountains (Deuteronomy 32:22).

Upon the wicked He shall rain snares, fire and brimstone, and an horrible tempest: this shall be the portion of their cup (Psalm 11:6).

WALKING—*Progress:* Living in (being led by) the Spirit; living in sin. **Difficult Walking** = *Trials;* opposition.

This I say then, Walk in the Spirit, and ye shall not fulfil the lust of the flesh. ... If we live in the Spirit, let us also walk in the Spirit (Galatians 5:16,25).

This I say therefore, and testify in the Lord, that ye henceforth walk not as other Gentiles walk, in the vanity of their mind (Ephesians 4:17).

WALL—*Barrier:* Obstacle; defense; limitation; unbelief. (See FENCE.)

...By my God have I leaped over a wall [obstacle] (2 Samuel 22:30).

He shall recount his worthies: they shall stumble in their walk; they shall make haste to the wall thereof, and the defense shall be prepared (Nahum 2:5).

The rich man's wealth is his strong city, and as an high wall in his own conceit [he cannot be reached with the gospel because of the barrier of his pride] (Proverbs 18:11).

WALLET—See PURSE.

WASHBASIN—*Prayer:* Repentance; petition (to God); self-justification (as when Pilate washed his hands at Christ's trial [see Mt. 27:24]). (See BATHROOM, *Section 2.*)

Wash you, make you clean; put away the evil of your doings from before Mine eyes; cease to do evil (Isaiah 1:16).

O Jerusalem, wash thine heart from wickedness, that thou mayest be saved. How long shall thy vain thoughts lodge within thee? (Jeremiah 4:14)

WASHCLOTH—*Truth:* Doctrine; understanding. **Dirty Cloth** = *False Doctrine;* insincere apology; error. (See SOAP.)

> *Purge me with hyssop* [a branch used as a brush in cleansing], *and I shall be clean: wash me, and I shall be whiter than snow* (Psalm 51:7).

> *Now ye are clean through the word* [truth] *which I have spoken unto you* (John 15:3).

> *Who can bring a clean thing out of an unclean* [dirty washcloth]? *not one* (Job 14:4).

WATER—*Spirit:* Word, and therefore the Spirit of God, the spirit of man or the spirit of the enemy; unstable. **Stagnant, Muddy, or Polluted Water** = *Man's doctrines and ways;* iniquity; haughty spirit; unkind. **Troubled Water** = *Trouble;* worry; sorrow; healing. (See SWIMMING, FLOOD, and RIVER.)

> *The words of a man's mouth are as deep waters, and the wellspring of wisdom as a flowing brook* (Proverbs 18:4).

> *That He might sanctify and cleanse it with the washing of water by the word* (Ephesians 5:26).

> *Behold, the days come, saith the Lord God, that I will send a famine in the land, not a famine of bread, nor a thirst for water, but of hearing the words of the Lord* (Amos 8:11).

> *Unstable as water, thou shalt not excel...* (Genesis 49:4).

> *But the wicked are like the troubled sea, when it cannot rest, whose waters cast up mire and dirt* (Isaiah 57:20).

> *What man is like Job, who drinketh up scorning like water?* (Job 34:7)

WATER FOUNTAIN—*Spirit:* Words; spirit of man; Holy Spirit; salvation; source.

Doth a fountain send forth at the same place sweet water and bitter? Can the fig tree, my brethren, bear olive berries? either a vine, figs? so can no fountain both yield salt water and fresh (James 3:11-12).

…I am Alpha and Omega, the beginning and the end. I will give unto him that is athirst of the fountain of the water of life freely (Revelation 21:6).

For My people have committed two evils; they have forsaken Me the fountain of living waters, and hewed them out cisterns, broken cisterns [man's doctrines], *that can hold no water* (Jeremiah 2:13).

WATERMELON—*Fruit:* Refreshing; picnic. **Seeds** = *Words.* **Water** = *Spirit.* **Sweet** = *Strength.* **Green** = *Life.* **Red** = *Passion;* the fruit of good or evil works; the pleasures of sin. (See GARDENING.)

We remember the fish, which we did eat in Egypt [the world, i.e., sin] *freely; the cucumbers, and the melons, and the leeks, and the onions, and the garlic* ["the spice of (sinful) life"] (Numbers 11:5).

Therefore shall they eat of the fruit of their own [backsliding] *way…* (Proverbs 1:31).

Say ye to the righteous, that it shall be well with him: for they shall eat the fruit of their doings (Isaiah 3:10).

Death and life are in the power of the tongue: and they that love it [righteousness] *shall eat the fruit thereof* (Proverbs 18:21).

WATER WELL—*Source:* Heart; spirit of man; the Holy Spirit.

Keep thy heart [well] *with all diligence; for out of it are the issues of life* (Proverbs 4:23).

These [deceivers] *are wells without water…to whom the mist of darkness is reserved for ever* (2 Peter 2:17).

Jesus answered and said unto her, If thou knewest the gift of God, and who it is that saith to thee, Give Me to drink; thou wouldest have asked of Him, and He would have given thee living water. … Jesus answered and said unto her, Whosoever drinketh of this water shall thirst again: but whosoever drinketh of the water that I shall give him shall never thirst; but the water that I shall give him shall be in him a well of water springing up into everlasting life (John 4:10,13-14).

WEDDING—See MARRIAGE.

WEEDS—*Unkept:* Works of the flesh; sin; neglect; laziness; worry; the fullness of iniquity (if they are gone to seed). (See SEED.)

And the Lord God took the man, and put him into the garden of Eden to dress it and to keep it (Genesis 2:15).

I went by the field of the slothful, and by the vineyard of the man void of understanding; and, lo, it was all grown over with thorns, and nettles had covered the face thereof, and the stone wall thereof was broken down (Proverbs 24:30-31).

The waters compassed me about, even to the soul: the depth closed me round about, the weeds [fears, worries] *were wrapped about my head* (Jonah 2:5).

But in the fourth generation they shall come hither again: for the iniquity [weeds, i.e., works of the flesh] *of the Amorites is not yet full* [mature, i.e., gone to seed, therefore only capable of reproducing itself] (Genesis 15:16).

WESTERN—*Frontier (as in "the wild West," or a western movie, etc.):* Pioneering spirit; spiritual warfare; boldness; challenge.

When thou comest nigh unto a city to fight against it, then proclaim [the gospel of] *peace unto it* (Deuteronomy 20:10).

Yet there shall be a space between you and it, about two thousand cubits by measure [i.e., use mature judgment]*: come not near unto it, that ye may know the way by which ye must go: for ye have not passed this way heretofore* (Joshua 3:4).

WIND—*Spirit or Doctrine (Therefore, wind can mean "the spirit of a doctrine."):* Holy Spirit; demonic or strong opposition (as in "a strong wind"); idle words. (See STORM.)

That we henceforth be no more children, tossed to and fro, and carried about with every wind of doctrine... (Ephesians 4:14).

The wind bloweth where it listeth, and thou hearest the sound thereof, but canst not tell whence it cometh, and whither it goeth: so is every one that is born of the Spirit (John 3:8).

And suddenly there came a sound from heaven as of a rushing mighty wind, and it filled all the house where they were sitting. ... And they were all filled with the Holy Ghost, and began to speak with other tongues, as the Spirit gave them utterance (Acts 2:2,4).

How long wilt thou speak these things? and how long shall the words of thy mouth be like a strong wind? (Job 8:2)

And the Lord said unto Satan, Behold, all that he [Job] hath is in thy power.... And, behold, there came a great [or strong] wind from the wilderness, and smote the four corners of the house, and it fell upon the young men, and they are dead... (Job 1:12,19).

WINDOW—*Revealed:* Truth; prophecy; revelation; understanding; avenue of blessing; exposed; an unguarded opening for a thief to enter.

And it came to pass...that Abimelech king of the Philistines looked out at a window, and saw, and, behold, Isaac was sporting with Rebekah [and he realized she was] his wife (Genesis 26:8).

And that lord answered the man of God, and said, Now, behold, if the Lord should make windows in heaven, might such a thing [blessing] be? And he said, Behold, thou shalt see it with thine eyes, but shalt not eat thereof (2 Kings 7:19).

They shall run to and fro in the city; they shall run upon the wall, they shall climb up upon the houses; they shall enter in at the windows like a thief (Joel 2:9).

WINE (or Strong Drink)—*Intoxicant:* Strong emotion (such as joy, anger, hate, or sorrow); Spirit (of God or spirit of man); revelation; truth; witchcraft; delusion; mocker. **Drinking Wine With Someone** = *Spiritual fellowship;* communion.

And be not drunk with [natural] wine, wherein is excess; but be filled with the [new wine of the] Spirit (Ephesians 5:18).

And no man putteth new wine [revelation] into old bottles [tradition, wrong or obsolete doctrine]; else the new wine will burst the bottles, and be spilled, and the bottles shall perish. But new wine [truth] *must be put into new bottles* [doctrines]; *and both are preserved* (Luke 5:37-38).

Give strong drink [the knowledge of God] *unto him that is ready to perish, and wine* [the Spirit of joy] *unto those that be of heavy hearts* [See Isaiah 61:3.] (Proverbs 31:6).

Others mocking said, These men are full of new wine. ... For these are not drunken, as ye suppose... But this is that which was spoken by the prophet Joel; and it shall come to pass in the last days, saith God, I will pour out of My Spirit upon all flesh: and your sons and your daughters shall prophesy, and your young men shall see visions, and your old men shall dream dreams (Acts 2:13,15-17).

For they eat the bread of wickedness, and drink the wine [spirit] *of violence* (Proverbs 4:17).

For their vine is of the vine of Sodom, and of the fields of Gomorrah: their grapes are grapes of gall, their clusters [and therefore their wines] *are bitter* (Deuteronomy 32:32).

Wine is a mocker, strong drink is raging: and whosoever is deceived thereby is not wise (Proverbs 20:1).

The cup of blessing which we bless, is it not the communion of the blood of Christ? The bread which we break, is it not the communion of the body of Christ? (1 Corinthians 10:16)

WINGS—*Spirit:* Minister (prophet); Holy Spirit; shelter; demon. (See BIRD.)

Ye have seen what I did unto the Egyptians, and how I bare you on eagles' wings, and brought you unto Myself [Compare Hosea 12:13: "And by a prophet the Lord brought Israel out of Egypt, and by a prophet was he preserved."] (Exodus 19:4).

He shall cover thee with His feathers [Spirit], and under His wings shalt thou trust: His truth shall be thy shield and buckler (Psalm 91:4).

But they that wait upon the Lord shall renew their strength; they shall mount up with wings as eagles; they shall run, and not be weary; and they shall walk, and not faint (Isaiah 40:31).

But unto you that fear My name shall the Sun of righteousness arise with healing in His wings [Spirit]; and ye shall go forth, and grow up as calves of the stall (Malachi 4:2).

WINTER—*Barren:* Death; dormant; waiting; cold (unfriendly). (See SNOW.)

The harvest is past, the summer is ended [and winter has come], and we are not saved (Jeremiah 8:20).

For ye shall be as an oak whose leaf fadeth, and as a garden that hath no water (Isaiah 1:30).

WOOD—*Life:* Temporary; flesh; humanity; carnal reasoning; lust; eternal (as in "a house made of cedars"); spiritual building material. (See TREE(S).)

Wherefore thus saith the Lord God of hosts, Because ye speak this word, behold, I will make My words in thy mouth fire, and this people wood, and it shall devour them (Jeremiah 5:14).

Where no wood is, there the fire goeth out: so where there is no talebearer [works of the flesh], the strife ceaseth. As coals are to burning coals, and wood to fire; so is a contentious man to kindle strife (Proverbs 26:20-21).

Now if any man build upon this foundation gold [wisdom], *silver* [knowledge], *precious stones* [the witness of God's Spirit], *wood* [carnal reasoning], *hay* [dead works], *stubble* [tradition] (1 Corinthians 3:12).

WRESTLING—*Striving:* Deliverance; resistance; persistence; trial; tribulation; controlling spirit (person) attempting to gain control. (See BOXING.)

And Jacob was left alone; and there wrestled a man [an angel] *with him until the breaking of the day. ... And he said, Let me go, for the day breaketh. And he said, I will not let thee go, except thou bless me. ... And he said, Thy name shall be called no more Jacob, but Israel: for as a prince hast thou power with God and with men, and hast prevailed* (Genesis 32:24,26,28).

For we wrestle not against flesh and blood, but against principalities, against powers, against the rulers of the darkness of this world, against spiritual wickedness in high places (Ephesians 6:12).

And the servant of the Lord must not strive [with men]; *but be gentle unto all men, apt to teach, patient* (2 Timothy 2:24).

Understanding Dreams

5B-3:13

More Books on Dreams

— **DREAMS IN THE SPIRIT, VOLUME 1**
by Bart Druckenmiller.
We all want to hear the word of the Lord. Nevertheless, many people don't. They limit how God speaks, not recognizing His voice throughout life's experiences, including dreams in the night and "daydreams" born of the Spirit. As a result, our lives lack vision and destiny. This book will introduce you to how God speaks through dreams and visions. It will give you hope that you, too, can learn to hear God's voice in your dreams and fulfill all that He speaks to you.
ISBN 1-56043-346-9

— **DREAMS IN THE SPIRIT, VOLUME 2**
by Bart Druckenmiller.
This book encourages the present generation on the importance of dreams, which are divinely inspired and given by God concerning personal destiny. Dreams and visions are windows to the supernatural. Through them, God allows you to see beyond the natural into the realms of glory, where Heaven's decisions about your personal life, destiny, and ministry are made. In this book, the author teaches how to hold onto and fulfill the dreams and visions God gives you...plus much more!
ISBN 1-56043-347-7

Additional copies of this book and other
book titles from DESTINY IMAGE are
available at your local bookstore.

Call toll-free: 1-800-722-6774

Send a request for a catalog to:

Destiny Image® Publishers, Inc.
P.O. Box 310
Shippensburg, PA 17257-0310

"Speaking to the Purposes of God for This
Generation and for the Generations to Come"

For a complete list of our titles,
visit us at www.destinyimage.com